PERSPECTIVES

A Multicultural Portrait of
World War I

By Michael V. Uschan

BENCHMARK BOOKS

MARSHALL CAVENDISH
NEW YORK

Cover: A group of African-American officers pose in 1918 with a French girl whose country they had come to free from the Germans. African-American soldiers fought well in the Great War (World War I), but they were forced to serve in segregated units. Their commanding officers were often whites because the army did not often promote African-Americans.

Benchmark Books
Marshall Cavendish Corporation
99 White Plains Road
Tarrytown, New York 10591-9001, U.S.A.

© Marshall Cavendish Corporation, 1996

Edited, designed, and produced by Water Buffalo Books, Milwaukee

Editorial consultant: Richard Taylor, History Department (Adjunct), the University of Wisconsin-Parkside

Picture Credits: © The Bettmann Archive: 9, 12, 16-17, 18, 19, 20, 21, 28, 30, 32, 33, 35, 36, 40, 43, 51, 60, 61, 62, 64-65; © Reuters/Bettmann: 8; © UPI/Bettmann: Cover, 6, 15 (both), 22, 24, 26, 27 (both), 34, 37, 38, 39, 42, 45, 46, 47, 48, 50, 52, 53, 56, 58, 67, 69, 70, 73

Library of Congress Cataloging-in-Publication Data

Uschan, Michael V.
    A multicultural portrait of World War I / by Michael V. Uschan
        p.   cm. -- (Perspectives)
    Includes bibliographical references and index.
    ISBN 0-7614-0054-0 (lib. bdg. : alk. paper)
    1. World War, 1914-1918--United States--Juvenile literature. 2. Multiculturalism--United States--Juvenile Books. I.
  Title. II. Series: Perspectives (Benchmark Books (Firm))
    D580.U73   1995
    959.4'0973--dc20   95-11035
                                                          CIP
                                                          AC

To PS – MS
To my wife, Barbara, with love, for standing by my side through *WWI* and all the other battles of my life – MVU

Printed in Malaysia
Bound in the U.S.A.

CONTENTS

About *Perspectives*

Perspectives is a series of multicultural portraits of events and topics in U.S. history. Each volume examines these events and topics not only from the perspective of the white European-Americans who make up the majority of the U.S. population, but also from that of the nation's many people of color and other ethnic minorities, such as African-Americans, Asian-Americans, Hispanic-Americans, and American Indians. These people, along with women, have been given little attention in traditional accounts of U.S. history. And yet their impact on historical events has been great.

The terms *American Indian, Native American, Hispanic-American, Latino, Anglo-American, Black, African-American,* and *Asian-American,* like *European-American* and *white,* are used by the authors in this series to identify people of various national origins. Labeling people is a serious business, and what we call a group depends on many things. For example, a few decades ago it was considered acceptable to use the words *colored* or *Negro* to label people of African origin. Today, these words are outdated and often a sign of ignorance or outright prejudice. Some even consider *Black* less acceptable than *African-American* because it focuses on a person's skin color rather than national origins. And yet *Black* has many practical uses, especially to describe people whose origins are not only African but Caribbean or Latin American as well.

If we must label people, it's better to be as specific as possible. That is a goal of *Perspectives* — to be as precise and fair as possible in the labeling of people by race, ethnicity, national origin, or other factors, such as gender, sexual orientation, or disability. When necessary and possible, Americans of Mexican origin will be called *Mexican-Americans.* Americans of Irish origin will be called *Irish-Americans,* and so on. The same goes for American Indians: When possible, specific Indians are identified by their tribal names, such as the Winnebago or *Mohawk.* But in a discussion of various Indian groups, tribal origins may not always be entirely clear, and so it may be more practical to use *American Indian,* a term that has widespread use among Indians and non-Indians alike.

Even within a group, individuals may disagree over the labels they prefer for their group: *Black* or *African-American? Hispanic* or *Latino? American Indian* or *Native American? White, Anglo,* or *European-American?* Different situations often call for different labels. The labels used in *Perspectives* represent an attempt to be fair, accurate, and perhaps most importantly, to be mindful of what people choose to call *themselves.*

A Note About *World War I*

World War I was important in U.S. history because it marked the nation's debut as a major global power. Up until the war, the United States had been overshadowed by European countries culturally, economically, militarily, and politically. The war gave the United States a new identity as a world leader.

The conflict also had a tremendous impact at home. One of the greatest effects was the migration of African-Americans from the South to northern cities. They were searching for a better life than they had in the South, where racism denied them many rights and they experienced lynchings, beatings, and other acts of violence. Blacks flocked by the tens of thousands to take new jobs the war had created. They found that racism existed in the North as well, although generally the conditions were better than what they had left behind.

Another domestic effect of the war was the paranoia that resulted in discrimination against German-Americans and other immigrants whose native countries were fighting against the United States. This occurred even when there was no cause to fear their loyalty. After the war, this antiforeign feeling continued to grow, resulting in restrictive immigration policies. A more positive effect was that the war provided new economic opportunities for many immigrants. For example, for the first time Mexican-Americans moved to northern cities in significant numbers. And hundreds of thousands of women entered the work force for the first time, especially after U.S. soldiers went to war overseas.

The greatest tragedy of World War I was that the countries involved failed to learn many lessons from a conflict that claimed the lives of more than 8.5 million soldiers and some 22 million civilians. The Great War, as it was then called, started because of resentments over past armed conflicts, greed for more territory, ethnic rivalry, and diplomatic plotting and maneuvering. Underlying these root causes was the hatred so many people had for other countries, nationalities, or ethnic groups. World War I only created more hatred, and it led to World War II just two decades later, when the participants lined up on almost the same sides and started fighting again.

By the final years of the twentieth century, the world, and the United States with it, has still not successfully come to terms with the problems of racism, discrimination, and ethnic hatred. Throughout the 1990s, the United States has once again turned to restrictive policies to stem the tide of new immigration, and a backlash has started against many new immigrants and foreign business interests. In Europe, the same ethnic antagonisms that unleashed World War I have resurfaced in places like Serbia, Croatia, and Bosnia-Herzegovina, all of which merged to form Yugoslavia after World War I but have become once again independent warring states following the dissolution of the Soviet Union and many of its satellite nations. The development of nuclear weaponry seems to have impressed upon the world how disastrous another global conflict would be. And yet, the tendency of history to repeat itself in small but significant ways remains one of the great and disturbing characteristics of humanity.

Austrian Archduke Franz Ferdinand and his wife, Duchess Sophie, are seated in the rear of this convertible as it is driven through Sarajevo on June 28, 1914. This historic photo was taken moments before a Serbian assassin jumped on the car's running board and fatally shot the royal couple. Their deaths were the political spark that ignited the Great War.

CHAPTER ONE

War's Beginning:
Assassination at Sarajevo - 1914

Sunday, June 28, 1914, dawned sunny and hot in Sarajevo. Sarajevo was the small, picturesque capital of Bosnia, which was then a province in the vast Austro-Hungarian Empire. It was a special day for Austrian Archduke Franz Ferdinand and his wife, Sophie, who were celebrating their fourteenth wedding anniversary. Franz Ferdinand was the heir to the throne of Austria-Hungary. The official reason for his basically meaningless visit was a chance to review Austrian troops, who were holding maneuvers near the border with neighboring Serbia. But the archduke also wanted to add some pomp and ceremony to the royal couple's personal celebration. They had come to Sarajevo expecting to hear the shouts and applause of adoring subjects. Instead, gunshots rang out and changed the course of history.

In a scene much like presidential motorcades today, the archduke and his wife were rolling through the gaily decorated streets in an open-air automobile, waving to people lining the streets. Scattered among the cheering throngs, however, were seven young Serbian nationalists. A nationalist is someone who often shows extreme devotion and loyalty to his or her country or ethnic group, and these young men were armed with pistols and crude bombs. They had decided on assassination as their way of making a political statement. They felt that Serbs in the provinces of Bosnia and Herzegovina should be freed from Austro-Hungarian rule so they could become part of a new nation, to be called Greater Serbia. The seven were students and workers, five of them under the age of twenty.

The archduke and his wife, holding a parasol to shield herself from the bright sun, were in the second of four cars in the procession. The first assassination attempt was a bomb thrown at the royal couple. It bounced away from their car and did little damage, although Sophie was hit in the face by a splinter when it exploded. The motorcade then sped to City Hall, where a furious Ferdinand demanded to know why he was being "received with bombs." When

Sarajevo, then and now

On the day after the assassination of Archduke Franz Ferdinand in Sarajevo, the capital of Bosnia, leaders around the world began considering the consequences of this rash act by a Serbian nationalist. But in Sarajevo itself, the bloody aftermath had already begun as some Croats and Muslims reacted as they always had in conflicts with rival Serbs — with violence. Croats and Muslims went on a rampage, destroying homes, businesses, schools, and other Serbian property. One man was killed, and fifty other people were wounded in the ethnic riot.

The bloody explosion of hatred died down in just a few hours that day in 1914, but anger and resentment stayed alive in the hearts of many Serbs, Croats, and Muslims. In fact, in 1992, the three ethnic groups began fighting each other again after Yugoslavia — the country they had all lived in since its creation after World War I — had fallen apart politically. The breakup split Yugoslavia into six smaller nations: Bosnia-Herzegovina, Serbia, Macedonia, Montenegro, Slovenia, and Croatia.

The fighting began in 1992 because Serbs were upset that Muslims and Croats wanted to withdraw from the new nation of Bosnia-Herzegovina, which the Serbs dominated militarily. But the resulting violence and ethnic genocide stemmed from the same feelings of nationalism and ethnic pride that had plagued Sarajevo in 1914. Each of the three groups wanted its own homeland, its own area where its people could rule themselves and feel free from interference by the other two groups.

The rioting against the Serbs in 1914 and the outbreak of hostilities nearly eighty years later, this time with the aggression coming from the Serbs, were both fueled by the hatred all three groups have for each other. Long years of conflict between them had created this hatred, and hatred is an emotion that is difficult to extinguish.

In 1914 in Sarajevo, a violent act that helped ignite a world war was met with more violence. In 1992, the three groups showed the world, once again, that they had not learned from the mistakes of the past.

the angry archduke finally cooled his legendary temper, he decided to visit a local hospital to check on any victims. It turned out to be a fatal mistake.

On the way, the driver of Franz Ferdinand's car made a wrong turn, putting him directly in the path of Gavrilo Princip, a Serbian assassin. Princip jumped on the car's running board and fired twice. One bullet hit Franz Ferdinand in the neck, the other struck his wife in the abdomen. The archduke muttered in German several times, "Es ist nichts [it is nothing]." But he was wrong — he and Sophie soon died of their wounds. Their deaths led to the first war to involve the entire world — a titanic, horrifying struggle that took the lives of more than 8.5 million soldiers and 22 million civilians. The conflict toppled royal dynasties, created new countries, and shifted the balance of world power. To the dismay of future generations, it also sowed the bitter seeds that led to World War II just a few decades later.

The Roots of War: Hatred, Greed, and the Desire for Freedom

Leon Trotsky, who in 1917 made his mark in history by helping lead the communist revolution in Russia, wrote that when the archduke got into his car that day in Sarajevo, "History had already poised its gigantic soldier's boot over the ant heap." The assassination, however, was not the main reason countries around the world began fighting in the Great War, as World War I was then called. It was, however, the spark that touched off smoldering resentments and hatreds that had existed in Europe for many years.

In the first years of the twentieth century, to most Americans and Europeans the world seemed a safe and secure place. Great advances were being made in science and technology, and the arts were flourishing in both Europe and the United States. There was growing optimism that a "modern world" was being created. Great Britain had a formidable navy, arrogantly ruling the seas and boasting of an empire "the sun never set on" because it encircled the globe. France, basking in a period of cultural refinement called the *"belle epoque,"* was the center of the world for painting and other arts. In the early 1870s, Germany, previously a handful of separate, rival states, had been united into one nation under the iron fist of Chancellor Otto von Bismarck. Germany was already becoming Europe's dominant industrial power and a military one as well. Across the Atlantic Ocean, the United States was flexing its muscles economically and politically, trying to find its place among the world's powers.

Otto von Bismarck, whose nickname was the Iron Chancellor. He was the political leader who unified the German Empire in the late nineteenth century.

But beneath the surface calm, Europe was a simmering cauldron of greed and hate that would soon boil over and engulf the world. At one time or another, the European countries had all made war on each other. Germany, for instance, had been victorious in the Franco-Prussian War of 1871. In the first years of the new century, France and Germany hated each other; they could hardly wait to fight again. Austria-Hungary and Serbia had long battled over territory that had formerly been controlled by the weakening Ottoman Empire. Several centuries earlier, this huge empire had stretched from Austria to Southern Arabia, but by 1914, its size had been reduced by numerous skirmishes with other nations.

Austria-Hungary had been one of the countries to take land from the Turkish Ottoman Empire in a series of wars at the beginning of the twentieth century. In 1908, Austria-Hungary had annexed Bosnia and Herzegovina. But the nation of Serbia wanted this land back because many Serbs lived there. Serbia, with backing from mighty Russia, almost went to war with Austria-Hungary over Bosnia and Herzegovina. The basis of the resentment between the two countries was that Slavic peoples, such as the Serbs, wanted to be free of rule by the Austrians, a German-speaking people.

Germanic and Slavic ethnic groups — longtime rivals

Leading up to the Great War, the ethnic rivalry that created the most tension in Europe was that between the Germanic and Slavic peoples.

Slavs are members of the largest single body of Europeans linked by ethnic heritage and language. They are divided into three groups: the east Slavs (mainly Russians, Ukrainians, and Belorussians); the west Slavs (chiefly Poles, Czechs, and Slovaks); and the south Slavs (including Serbs, Croats, Slovenes, and Macedonians).

Members of many of the Slavic ethnic groups lived in the Austro-Hungarian Empire. In the years before the war started, they were unhappy at being ruled by the Hapsburgs, a German family that reigned in Austria from 1278 to the end of the Great War. In 1867, Austria and the kingdom of Hungary united, with the Hapsburgs ruling what was known as the Dual Monarchy until the end of the war in 1918.

Austria-Hungary was a huge, sprawling empire of 261,000 square miles that had a population in 1914 of about 52 million people. Its two main ethnic groups were 12 million people of German heritage, who lived mainly in the area that today makes up the nation of Austria, and 10 million Magyars, who were located in the central plains of modern-day Hungary. But the empire also included millions of Slavic people, including about 8.5 million Czechs and Slovaks; 7.5 million Croats, Slovenes, and Serbs, who were known collectively as Yugoslavs (or south Slavs); some 5 million Poles; and about 4 million Ukrainians.

Russia, a Slavic nation, and the Germanic nations had contended with one another for power for centuries. A new factor in the rivalry was the growing desire by Slavic groups in Austria-Hungary to be ruled by themselves. For instance, Serbs living in Bosnia, a province of Austria-Hungary, wanted to be united with the neighboring country of Serbia.

As early as 1912, German General Helmuth von Moltke had predicted, "A European war is bound to come sooner or later, and [it will] . . . in the last resort, be a struggle between Teuton [the Germans] and Slav." He noted that "the attack must come from the Slavs" so Germany would be justified in going to war. The assassination of Austrian Archduke Franz Ferdinand provided that excuse for war. In this way, ethnic rivalry helped nations choose sides in the war.

In the years leading up to World War I, many European nations were being torn from within as people demanded more political freedom from dictatorial monarchies, that is, from being ruled by kings and queens. And widespread feelings of nationalism — the desire of ethnic and racial groups to control their own lands — were also starting to create internal unrest. When the Great War began, it was seen by many as a clash of royal empires. The irony is that the German, Russian, and Austrian empires, and the royal families that ruled them, all vanished in the ashes of the conflict. And after the war, the colonial empires that European countries had built up all over the world began to crumble as well, as nations and ethnic groups began to fight for the right to govern themselves.

In 1914, then, many factors were creating terrible tensions between nations. Responding to these tensions, Europeans began to prepare for the bloodiest war the world had ever seen.

The Opening Moves

On July 28, 1914, a month after the double assassination, Austria-Hungary declared war on Serbia. The declaration came by telegram, the first time this communications technology had been used for such a purpose. There had been some halfhearted negotiations between the two countries, but from the start, Austria-Hungary had wanted to punish Serbia. That single declaration of war was like knocking over the first in a long line of dominoes, and other nations lined up quickly. Many countries had signed secret pacts years earlier in which they pledged to come to each other's defense in time of war. Thus, once a few countries began fighting, many other nations also went to war to honor their commitments.

The initial lineup pitted the Allies — France, Great Britain, Belgium, and Russia — against the Central Powers of Germany, Austria-Hungary, and Turkey. Before World War I ended in 1918, however, many other countries became involved. Fighting spread to European colonies in Africa, Asia, and the Pacific. Around the world, nations fought to defend their colonies or to win new land from the opposing side. Japan, for instance, declared war against Germany on August 23, 1914, as an excuse to take that country's holdings in China. Japan wanted more territory in China in order to increase its economic and political power. For its part, China did not care about the war in Europe either but was worried that if it did not go to war against the Central Powers, the Allies would reward Japan with huge chunks of land in China for helping them win the Great War.

Other countries also saw it in their best interests to take sides. In 1915, Italy joined the Allies, and Bulgaria sided with the Central Powers, also out of greed for more land. Throughout the Great War, many countries that seemed to have no real interest in the war joined both sides. Honduras was the very last. The small Central American nation declared war against Germany on July 19, 1918, just three months before fighting ended.

The war began on August 4, 1914, when five German army divisions invaded neutral Belgium. This tiny country's only sin was that its easily negotiable terrain offered the easiest path for Germany to attack France. The Germans, in fact, had been mapping out this plan of attack for many years. It was named the Von Schlieffen Plan, after General Alfred von Schlieffen, who had created it. In fact, Germany would use the same route to invade France in World War II. Like the claws of a giant beast, the five armies sliced through Belgium and lumbered downward through northern France. The invaders overwhelmed the French and British forces that stood in their path and pushed them back.

After losing almost all of Belgium and part of northern France, the Allies finally regrouped. When the two sides collided in early September in the Battle of the Marne (named after the nearby Marne River in northeastern France), the Allies were finally able to stop the German advance. Drained of strength by the end of September, the two sides paused from active fighting and began fortifying their battle lines. By December, they had established the trenches, ramparts, and fortifications along the line that became known as the Western Front. This front began at the North Sea and zigzagged five hundred miles east and south across Belgium and France to the border of Switzerland. Although the combatants had not realized it, the Battle of the Marne was the decisive one of the war. Germany's first onslaught had been its only chance to defeat France. When the attack failed, a stalemate developed. After that, it was only a matter of time before the Allies' superior strength —with the addition of U.S. forces in 1917 — would prevail.

There was one more major offensive on the Western Front in 1914 — the First Battle of Ypres. On October 20, the Germans attacked in an attempt to capture this small Belgian town, which was a valuable communications center. Before the war was over, the two sides battled twice more over Ypres, and its ground soaked up the blood of more than 1 million dead and wounded human beings. In this first conflict, nearly 250,000 soldiers died. The Germans, who suffered 130,000 deaths, were beaten back in a battle that raged through November 22. Both sides then settled in for the winter in what became the start of four years of trench warfare. This term, coined in 1917, means warfare in which the opposing sides attack and counterattack from permanent trenches, usually protected with barbed wire.

German soldiers making themselves comfortable in a trench. For months at a time, soldiers on both sides lived and fought in these makeshift fortifications. They became so accustomed to living in them for long periods that trenches began to seem like home.

For the rest of the war, the Western Front was fairly stable. Even though both sides mounted repeated offensives that cost millions of soldiers their lives, neither was able to make any significant breakthroughs or gains during the war. The soldiers were basically stuck in the trenches for months, living, dying, and suffering there terribly. They froze in winter, lived in a sea of mud when it rained, and were pounded mercilessly by artillery they had no hope of silencing. They endured the anxiety of being separated by only a short distance from enemies who, at any time, could come pouring out of opposing trenches to attack. "No man's land," the war-ravaged terrain between the trenches, could be several miles wide, or it could be no more than a few hundred yards. Sometimes the trenches were so close that opposing soldiers carried on conversations by shouting at each other. They could even exchange Christmas greetings, something that really happened.

This static form of warfare was portrayed by German author Erich Maria Remarque in *All Quiet on the Western Front*, perhaps the greatest novel of World War I. In the following passage, a soldier praises the protection of the earth: "To no man does the earth mean so much as to the soldier . . . earth with thy folds and hollows, and holes, into which a man may fling himself and crouch down. In the spasm of terror, under the hailing of annihilation, in the bellowing death of the explosions, o' earth, thou grantest us . . . new-won life."

Another horror of trench warfare was that soldiers were often surrounded by their slain comrades, then forced to bury the dead in nearby, makeshift graves. In the book *Now It Can Be Told,* British war correspondent Philip Gibbs describes details of trench warfare. He wrote that he dared not report these details during the war because they would have destroyed British morale: "Lice crawled over [the dead] in legions. Human flesh, rotting and stinking, mere pulp, was pasted into the mudbanks. If they dug to get deeper cover their shovels went into the softness of dead bodies who had been their comrades. Scraps of flesh, booted legs, blackened hands, eyeless heads, came falling over them when the enemy trench-mortared their position or blew up a new mine-shaft."

The Central Powers also had to fight battles on their eastern borders, which became known as the Eastern Front. In August, they beat back a Russian invasion of the German state of East Prussia. At this same time, Austria-Hungary was attempting to invade Serbia, but Russia joined the Serbs and mauled Austria-Hungary in several battles to defeat the invaders. The Ottoman Empire had joined the Central Powers in hopes of gaining land when the Allies were defeated. It also hoped to get help with two other concerns: defending the long border it shared with Russia and fighting the British for land it controlled in the Middle East. The main Middle East campaigns took place in territory that includes the modern-day nations of Israel (then Palestine) and Iraq (then part of a region known as Mesopotamia).

In addition to the more than 8.5 million soldiers who died in the Great War, millions of innocent civilians were also killed, wounded, or brutalized as armies stormed through their homelands. Some countries also used the war to deal with internal problems. Among these were the Turkish leaders of the Ottoman Empire. At the outbreak of the war in 1914, the Ottoman Empire had a population of about 25 million. This included 10 million Turks and 6 million Arabs as well as large populations of Kurds, Greeks, and Armenians. The Turkish leaders began a campaign of widespread oppression of minorities and atrocities on a massive scale. People were forced to leave their homes, and entire villages were leveled. To the horror of the rest of the world, the Turks killed as many as 1million Armenians. The Ottoman Empire wanted to prevent the Armenians from helping Russia Additionally, the Armenians were Christian, and the Turks were Muslim; believers in the rival faiths had fought for centuries, and there was a great deal of hatred on both sides. The Turkish genocide against the Armenians became one of the war's most brutal and widespread atrocities.

The Melting Pot Divides over War

In the United States, initial reaction to the Great War was mixed, with many citizens siding with their ancestral homelands. Although most Americans felt the United States had no reason to become involved in the fighting, Germany, Serbia, France, and other nations began to recruit people from their country who had emigrated to the United States. Many immigrants had instilled a love of their homeland in their children, and recruiters played on those feelings. Serbian-Americans enlisted by the thousands, many never to return because they died in the war or stayed in Europe once the war was over. At the time

Americans wooed by propaganda

Before the Great War, the term *propaganda* referred to efforts by religious groups to spread their faith. But it took on a new meaning at the start of the Great War, as both the Allies and the Central Powers tried to woo the United States to their side. Propaganda became a political tool to further a cause, or to hurt someone else's, by spreading ideas, information, or rumors.

One of the tactics in this new approach was to print slanted news stories in German-American newspapers, which generally supported the Central Powers. These stories reported false claims of Allied war atrocities. The Allies, for their part, censored war coverage and controlled the flow of news back to the United States. Another tactic was to have celebrities in literature, science, and many other fields, from both the Allies and the Central Powers, make pleas to U.S. citizens to support their respective countries in the war. The statements blamed the other side for causing the war, accused enemy nations of brutality, and advised Americans that their cause was the one the United States should support.

Allied propagandists claimed that German soldiers had cut off the hands of Belgian children and crucified Canadian soldiers who were fighting on the British side. The Germans countered with claims that the French had dropped cholera germs into wells used by Germans and that a Belgian priest set up a machine gun behind an altar and killed German soldiers when they came to church. In an editorial on September 9, 1914, The *New York Time* stated, "This is the first press agents' war."

Sometimes these attempts at propaganda were downright silly. One report from the Allies claimed that the Germans were using dead bodies to make soap, grease, and fertilizer. The claim stemmed from a German newspaper story that referred to the use of "kadavers" for this purpose. Although the English word *cadaver* has its origin in the German language, the German word *kadaver* refers only to animal bodies and not human ones. A British propagandist picked up this report and made the Germans look like monsters, even though this was due to a mistake in translation.

Both sides did commit atrocities during the war, but many of the reports of battle and wartime brutality were more fiction than fact.

of the Great War, the country known today as Poland was divided, with parts of it controlled by Germany, Austria-Hungary, and Russia. Many Americans of Polish descent also went to war in order to fight for an independent Poland. Soldiers leaving for Europe sometimes paraded through U.S. cities, where local laws often required the U.S. flag to be shown if a foreign one was displayed. So, ironically, some soldiers who a few years later would fight against the United States marched off to war carrying the U.S. flag.

Many Americans sided immediately with the Allies because of their strong cultural bonds with Great Britain. But cities with large German populations, such as New York, Milwaukee, and St. Louis, held rallies to support the "Kaiser" — the term for German Emperor Wilhelm II. And Irish-Americans, who hated the English, cheered the Germans because they felt a German victory might allow Ireland to break free from English rule. In some cities, like Milwaukee, people had divided loyalties. German-born Oscar Ameringer, editor of the Socialist Party newspaper *Voice of the People*, reported that Polish-Americans were "fighting the battles of Poland in the twentieth and fourteenth wards of Milwaukee." In 1914, the same resentments that led Poles to fight against the Germans in the Great War had people of Polish and German descent battling each other in Milwaukee and other U.S. cities.

Some Americans were shocked that so many nations were all fighting at the same time, but many did not really care what was happening in Europe. Only the rich were able to travel to Europe, and most people did not know very much about current events in foreign countries like England and Germany, much less Serbia and Austria-Hungary. Even when the war did begin, newspapers were the only source of news. Radio and television had not been invented yet, and the newspaper reports lacked the sense of immediacy and emotional impact that these media create today for listeners and viewers. Also, the United States had been a self-sufficient nation for many years; its citizens worried more about their own problems than those of other countries. The one nearly universal sentiment in 1914 was that the war was terrible and should be stopped — preferably without the United States becoming involved. When the war began, President Woodrow Wilson decided the nation should remain neutral. He declared October 4, 1914, "Peace Sunday" and asked everyone to pray for peace. The next day the headline on the front page of the *New York Tribune* shouted: "Thousands Join in Plea of Universal Creed at President's Request."

Above: In 1915, two German-American women in San Francisco pound nails into a giant Iron Cross — a symbol of German bravery. All the nails were "sold" to contributors, and the money that was collected went to the German Relief Fund. The idea was to sell enough nails to completely cover the cross with the metal nail heads.

Americans also felt a sense of security because they were separated from the fighting by thousands of miles. They felt that the war would not have serious consequences for them. It was an illusion that was to be quickly shattered the next year when Americans started losing their lives in attacks by submarines.

Left: Passengers on the *Oceanic*, which in 1914 sailed from New York to Germany. Despite their jubilation, many of these immigrants were returning home to fight in the Great War. Some of them probably died in the fighting, never to return to the United States.

Members of a German submarine crew watch as a U.S. ship they had attacked sinks slowly into the sea. This painting by Willy Stower dramatically depicts this form of warfare, which horrified Americans and helped turn many against Germany. The sinking of the *Lusitania* in 1915 was one of the key events in the first year of the Great War.

CHAPTER TWO

The World Conflict Spreads - 1915

As the luxury liner *Lusitania* steamed majestically out of New York harbor on May 1, 1915, the Great War was only ten months old. The Germans had begun submarine warfare, and the silent, unseen predators were taking a heavy toll of ships from countries fighting against them. But as the *Lusitania* headed for Liverpool, England, the 1,924 people aboard seemed not to feel any threat of war. They were delighted to be sailing aboard a ship that was the first to be called a "floating hotel." Some passengers even boldly displayed a sign that read, "To Hell with the Kaiser and his U-Boats." U-boat is short for *Unterseeboot,* the German word for submarine. Maybe they had failed to read a notice the Imperial German Embassy had printed in newspapers that same day, directly beneath an advertisement for the ship's departure.

The message was simple — a war was going on. Any ship bound for an Allied port was "liable to destruction," and people making such a voyage did so "at their own risk." Passengers also might have been more worried if they had known the massive liner — 790 feet long and 30,000 tons — was a British ship secretly carrying gunpowder and other munitions purchased in the United States by Allied nations. Instead, the passengers were gaily looking forward to a luxurious ocean voyage.

Six days later, the *Lusitania* was steaming off the coast of Ireland, nearing its destination. Shortly after 2:00 P.M. another vessel arrived on the scene. This ship, however, was running *under* the ocean. It was the *U-20,* command-

The *Lusitania*, dwarfing the tugboats that escort it out of the New York harbor on its fateful final voyage. Just six days later, this luxurious ocean liner would sink beneath the ocean after being attacked without warning by a German submarine.

ed by Captain Karl Schwieger, who that day earned a medal by firing a single torpedo. It hit the *Lusitania* on the starboard side, right behind the bridge. Through his periscope, Schwieger saw the flames and smoke of the explosion. In his captain's log, he recorded the *Lusitania's* nightmarish final minutes. As the massive ship took on water, then started to twist over and begin to go under, frantic passengers and crew members tried to lower lifeboats. "Many boats crowded, come down bow first or stern first in water and immediately fill and sink," wrote Schwieger almost sadly, as if he regretted his action. "I could not have fired a second torpedo into this throng of humanity attempting to save themselves." As the *Lusitania* sank, the *U-20* slipped away to a hero's welcome in Germany. The destructive force of the torpedo, combined with explosions of the munitions on board, sent the *Lusitania* to the bottom in less than twenty minutes. The death toll was 1,198, including 128 Americans, mostly women and children. Victims included 63 infants and children; of the 35 babies aboard, only four were saved.

In a very real way, the *U-20* also sank Germany's fortunes in the war. The hate and anger it created marked a major shift in American sympathy toward the Allies. None of the new and terrible weapons unleashed in the war — not airplanes, tanks, or poison gas — scared Americans more or created more revulsion than submarines. Americans felt it was sneaky, if not downright evil, to silently slip up to an innocent ship — and a pleasure ship, at that — and sink it without warning. Because Great Britain's navy ruled the surface of the seas, Germany had no other choice than to use submarines to stop the flow of Allied war material from the "neutral" United States. But in the process of claiming power at sea, the Germans had outraged a nation.

Submarine Warfare Angers America

The next day, the *Register and Leader*, a newspaper in Des Moines, Iowa, ran an editorial that repeated the line, "The sinking of the *Lusitania* was deliberate murder." This editorial was typical of U.S. reaction, and many Americans wanted to go to war right away. So the nation was expectant when President Woodrow Wilson spoke in Philadelphia just a few days later (May 10) to about four thousand immigrants who had recently become U.S. citizens. Wilson said America must set a "special example" for the world and must work for peace. "There is such a thing," he said, "as a nation being so right that it does not need to convince others by force that it is right . . . there is such a thing as a man being too proud to fight."

Many people considered Wilson's comments vague. Those who called for war after the sinking of the *Lusitania* condemned his speech, while those who desired peace praised it for cooling down war fever in the United States. Wilson, who wanted the country to remain officially neutral, had accomplished what he wanted with his remarks. He had condemned the sinking, but he had not committed the United States to an armed conflict.

President Woodrow Wilson, the twenty-eighth U.S. president, served from 1913 to 1921.

Wilson: No idealist on race

Woodrow Wilson was considered a man of high ideals and morals in many matters, but the Virginia-born twenty-eighth president failed to live up to that reputation in race relations. During the 1912 campaign, in an effort to win the vote of African-Americans who had traditionally voted Republican, he had vowed to see "justice done to colored people in every matter." It was a promise he never kept.

On April 11, 1913, Postmaster General Albert S. Burleson proposed in a cabinet meeting that African-Americans who worked for the federal government be segregated. Wilson did not oppose the plan. So for the first time since the Civil War, African-American federal workers were forced to work in separate areas from whites in their workplaces. The African-Americans also had to use separate restrooms and restaurants.

Because of this reversal of government support for African-Americans, federal postal and treasury officials in the South felt a new freedom to fire or demote Black workers. The Atlanta postmaster soon discharged thirty-five African-Americans, and an Internal Revenue collector in Georgia remarked, "A Negro's place is in the cornfield."

Yet Wilson saw nothing wrong. In response to protests, he wrote that he "honestly thought segregation (in federal offices) to be in the interest of the colored people as exempting them from friction and criticism." He said that "a number of colored men with whom we have consulted have agreed with us in this judgment."

In general in the early 1900s, African-Americans found themselves in a worse position than at any time since the end of the Civil War. Booker T. Washington, who was born into slavery but became a renowned educator and civil rights leader, said he had never seen his people so "discouraged and embittered" by the attitude of a presidential administration.

Oswald Garrison Villard, one of the founders of the National Association for the Advancement of Colored People (NAACP), later wrote that "not one thing was done by Woodrow Wilson or his administration to ameliorate the condition of the Negro."

Jane Addams, one of the leaders of the peace movement during the Great War, was criticized for opposing U.S. involvement.

Women's groups were at the forefront of the fight to keep the United States out of the war. Jane Addams, the first U.S. woman to win the Nobel Peace Prize, was perhaps the nation's leading spokesperson in this cause. In March of 1915 in a meeting attended by people from all over the nation, she helped found the Women's Peace Party. Addams was named president of this group. She also became head of the International Congress of Women, which met in April of 1915 in The Hague, Netherlands, to plead for an end to the war. Addams and other representatives met with leaders from both sides in the conflict, but she failed to get them to agree to end the fighting. When Addams returned home in August, she was attacked by newspapers for taking part in the peace effort. In response, she complained the American press was trying "to make pacifist activity . . . so absurd that it would be absolutely without influence."

Most newspapers had favored U.S. participation in the war since its beginning in 1914. For example, the *New York Herald's* headline the day after the sinking of the *Lusitania* was: "What a Pity Theodore Roosevelt Is Not President!" Newspapers helped make the former president the leader of those who want-

Jane Addams fought for peace

In 1931, Jane Addams became the first American woman to receive the Nobel Peace Prize when she was honored for her work to help immigrants and the poor. Addams was the founder of Hull House in Chicago, a settlement house that provided poor people and immigrants with the services they needed to improve their lives. Addams also helped set up facilities in other cities to provide medical services, child care, legal aid, and education for people who desperately needed them.

Although revered for her social work, Addams was hated by many during the Great War because she was a leader in the movement to keep the United States out of the fighting. It was a difficult stand for Addams to take. As U.S. opinion grew more and more favorable to war, Addams began to question whether it was right

to oppose something so many people advocated. "[Has] the individual or a very small group the right to stand against millions of his fellow countrymen? Is there not a great value in mass judgment and in instinctive mass enthusiasm . . . ?" she wrote.

Despite the personal pain it caused, Addams stayed true to her beliefs — and she suffered because of that. Retaliation even included harassment by the city health department in Chicago, which on many occasions falsely cited Hull House for "inefficient sanitary service." The citations were issued strictly to punish her for her antiwar views.

But Addams continued her life's work of helping others. And by the time of her death in 1935 at age seventy-four, she was once again revered by Americans.

ed to go to war. Roosevelt had become famous during the Spanish-American War, when he led a group of soldiers that earned the nickname "the Rough Riders." He said Germany must be held to "strict accountability" for the loss of life in the *Lusitania* incident. Even more angrily, Roosevelt added that it was "inconceivable we should refrain from action . . . we owe it not only to humanity but to our own national self-respect." Supreme Court Chief Justice Edward D. White commented, "I wish I were thirty years younger, I would go to Canada and enlist."

Secretary of State William Jennings Bryan, the legendary Democratic leader and orator, was an advocate of strict neutrality and wanted to keep the United States out of the war. After the sinking of the *Lusitania*, the United States and Germany began negotiations over submarine warfare. Bryan encouraged the United States to remain neutral in the talks, but he became upset over the harshness of the U.S. attitude toward Germany. Bryan felt the United States had been much more lenient with Great Britain shortly after the war started. At that time, Britain had prevented U.S. ships from delivering supplies to German ports. Bryan felt this was a violation of U.S. rights, and he disliked the British arrogance about controlling the seas. He became so angry over the U.S. attitude that on June 8, 1915, he resigned from his post and became a leader in the pacifist movement.

The United States continued negotiating with Germany until a compromise was reached on May 4, 1916. Germany agreed not to fire on merchant or passenger ships until the ships had been warned and passengers had been given a chance to escape. The agreement, however, lasted less than a year.

William Jennings Bryan, a legendary political leader for many years who was U.S. secretary of state when the Great War began. In 1915, he resigned his position in President Wilson's cabinet because he opposed U.S. involvement in the war. He felt the president was favoring the Allies.

Preparing for War

In 1915, the political fight was just starting over how well prepared the United States was to either defend itself or fight another country, if that ever became necessary. Roosevelt and other leaders of the Preparedness Movement argued that the United States needed to strengthen its weak armed forces, even if it was not going to war. In 1914, the United States had a strong navy, but its army numbered only about 200,000. Having the United States too weak to defend itself, claimed Roosevelt, "represents national emasculation." The Preparedness Movement was a strong one, and Wilson finally relented. In December 1915, he authorized creation of a new volunteer force that within three years would boost the armed forces to more than 670,000.

Chemical warfare is born

On April 22, 1915, French troops on the Western Front at Ypres were amazed to see greenish yellow clouds floating along the ground toward them from the German lines. They watched the strangely beautiful mist, unaware that it was deadly chlorine gas. When they began to breathe the terrible fumes, a horrible new form of warfare had been unleashed on the world.

The gas clogged their lungs, making them cough so hard they vomited, passed out, and died from lack of oxygen. The gas attack created total panic among some fifteen thousand soldiers, many of them Africans in the French Colonial Corps who had been recruited to defend the country that had enslaved their own. Those who could, fled, leaving a gap in the Allied lines more than four miles long.

The Germans made it to within twenty-five hundred yards of the town of Ypres before Canadian troops and British reserves repelled them. The German soldiers, afraid of the gas themselves, had advanced so slowly that Allied soldiers were able to come up to fill the gap. And the German high command, underestimating the effectiveness of the new

weapon, had not allocated enough troops for the offensive. So even though the gas attack was a success, the Germans failed to take Ypres.

The Germans had experimented with gas on the Eastern Front against the Russians earlier in 1915. The attack at Ypres, however, marked its official debut in war and quickly convinced both sides of its merits. The Allies and Central Powers both employed this new weapon, and as the war progressed, chlorine and tear gas gave way to the more deadly mustard and phosgene gas. The chemicals were released from cylinders, as at Ypres, or delivered by artillery shells.

During the war, chemical warfare resulted in one million medical casualties and more than seventy-nine thousand deaths. Gas masks — which looked either funny or horrible, depending on your point of view — quickly became a standard part of any soldier's armament. Although most nations have since outlawed chemical warfare, there were claims that Iraq tried to use chemicals against U.S. troops in 1991 during the war in the Persian Gulf.

As 1915 ended, Wilson was still opposed to war, even though more and more people were calling for U.S. entry into the conflict. But the United States had not yet been drawn into war, and that would become Wilson's campaign cry as he ran for reelection in 1916.

War – The Second Year

The Germans adopted a defensive strategy on the Western Front in 1915, while the Allies mounted several major offensives. The Allies gained little ground and lost soldiers by the tens of thousands. In February and March, the French made repeated attacks on German trenches in Champagne, a district in France. They won only five hundred yards at a cost of 50,000 dead. A joint Allied offensive in September along the German lines in Champagne was even bloodier, with 242,000 deaths for the Allies and 141,000 for the Germans. The Allies gained a little ground, but at a huge cost in lives. On April 22, the Germans made military history when they used chlorine gas for the first time on the Western Front, unleashing it in an attack at Ypres. Chemical warfare quickly became a standard weapon in the arsenal of both the Allies and the Central Powers.

On the Eastern Front, the Germans enjoyed great success, capturing the area that today makes up the nation of Poland and taking 750,000 Russian prisoners. The army of Austria-Hungary, with help from Germany and newly recruited Bulgaria, successfully invaded Serbia in October. The defeated Serbian Army was forced to flee over the Albanian mountains but came back to fight later in the war. Italy joined the Allies in 1915 and started an offensive eastward against the Austrians. But the fighting was practically a stalemate through a series of battles waged at the Isonzo River through 1916.

The Great War Spreads to European Colonies

The Great War circled the globe in 1915 as fighting was carried to European colonies in other parts of the world. During this period, the homelands of many people in Asia, India, the Pacific, and Africa were European colonies. One area greatly affected by World War I was Africa. The British and French invaded the German colonies of Togoland (known today as Togo) and Kamerun (Cameroon), and the new white-controlled government of South Africa moved to occupy the German colony of South-West Africa (Namibia). One conflict that lasted the entire war was the battle for German East Africa (Malawi). Most of the soldiers in these battles were

Colonialism in Africa

The Great War became a global conflict because the European nations involved in the fighting had possessions around the world. By 1914, European countries had been establishing colonies for centuries. The United States, remember, started out as thirteen separate British colonies before they won their own fight for freedom.

Colonialism (sometimes called imperialism) is the term for domination of one country by another, stronger nation, usually for the purpose of economic exploitation. In the late 1870s, European nations had begun conquering large portions of Africa. The push for new colonies in Africa was caused by discoveries of great mineral wealth, mainly diamonds and gold. Great Britain, Germany, Italy, France, and other European countries all established African colonies.

European leaders justified colonial rule by saying they were trying to civilize supposedly backward nations. This included efforts to force native populations to convert to Christianity. But by the turn of the century, many Africans were rejecting a religion dominated by whites, and the African Christian movement had begun. This brand of Christianity emphasized African nationalism.

During the Great War, the most famous African Christian rebel was John Chilembwe of Nyasaland (now Malawi), a British colony. In 1915, Chilembwe led his followers in a brief rebellion against Great Britain that was spurred by the fact that Africans were being forced to fight during the Great War in Europe and even in Africa, where they battled African soldiers recruited by other European nations. Chilembwe, who said he wanted to "strike a blow and die," started a small-scale rebellion. But his rebellion was defeated, and he did die — he was shot by British soldiers while trying to escape to Mozambique.

Africans forced to fight by the European powers who controlled their countries. Up to one million Kenyans and Tanzanians were forced to serve as porters for European armies fighting in eastern Africa, and as many as one hundred thousand died from disease, malnutrition, and overwork. The fighting also devastated civilian populations in African nations where fighting spread.

The Swahili word for soldier is *askari*, and the Germans who ruled in the eastern part of Africa forcibly recruited thousands of *askari* from native populations they had themselves conquered. Even worse, many Africans wound up fighting far from home in the trenches in France and Belgium. The French recruited more than 150,000 African soldiers, and as many as 30,000 died in battle. While Africans were dying for France in Europe, Frenchmen were consolidating their country's vast colonial holdings in Africa. When Germany was defeated in the Great War, the Allies divided up its possessions, including those in Africa.

The fighting even spread to China, where in 1914, the Japanese attacked German holdings in Kiachow, which included about two hundred square miles in the Chinese province of Shantung. Joined by British forces from Hong Kong, the Japanese defeated German troops. Japan had joined the fighting to get more possessions in China, but after the war, it was denied German holdings in Shantung. The war was also carried to islands Germany controlled in the Pacific. In 1914, Australian, British, and Japanese warships hunted down German ships, while soldiers from Australia and New Zealand captured the islands from the small contingents of German soldiers guarding them.

From the start of the war, the Turkish Ottoman Empire had battled Russia along its border with the present-day countries of Armenia and Azerbaijan. In 1915, the Ottoman Empire also began fighting against the British in the Mid-

Soldiers in the Chinese army drill in 1917. Even though China was thousands of miles away from the main conflict, it declared war on the Central Powers because fighting had spread to territory Germany controlled within China. It was in this way that a European conflict spread around the world.

dle East in Palestine (present-day Israel), Mesopotamia (Iraq), and Egypt. But Arab tribes in that region rebelled against the Turks and joined the Allies. The Arab uprising was sparked by the fabled T. E. Lawrence, a Welsh-born British scholar-soldier who lived and fought with the Arabs, earning the nickname "Lawrence of Arabia" and a wealth of fame, fortune, and notoriety as an adventurer. Although the rebellion benefited the Allies, it was really a war by the Arabs to overthrow Turkish rule of their land. Great Britain relied on many soldiers from India to fight in the Middle East, recruiting some eight hundred thousand from that British colony. A large part of the population in India was Muslim, however, and the use of troops from India against the Turks, who were also Muslim, was unpopular. Thousands of Indian soldiers died, some in combat but many more from disease and the effects of warfare in a desert climate.

"Hyphenated-Americans" and Racism

The Great War had begun to create changes in life in the United States. One of the most dramatic was the increased fear Americans had of immigrants, especially those from countries involved in the war. Former president Theodore Roosevelt led a movement that backed "100 percent Americanism" and was critical of what he termed "hyphenated-Americans." He said the leaders of the "hyphenated-American movement in this country . . . play the part of traitors, pure and simple." He added that the United States could not "endure half American and half foreign. The hyphen is incompatible with patriotism." By "hyphenated-Americans," Roosevelt meant immigrants who still felt some loyalty to their former homelands. He felt that people who immigrated to the United States should consider themselves Americans and be totally loyal to the U.S. government. His comments were directed mainly at Americans of Austrian and German descent who backed the Central Powers and were trying to keep the U.S. out of the war. The attitudes expressed by Roosevelt, however, wound up increasing suspicion and negative feelings toward all immigrants.

Not all of this suspicion was misplaced, however. At the same time that the Central Powers were trying to enlist U.S. support, they were undertaking a massive spying campaign in the United States that included acts of violence and sabotage. On July 15, 1915, two U.S. Secret Service agents gained possession of documents confirming that Germans had allocated more than 27 million dollars to be spent in the United States for the cause of "intrigue, conspiracy, and propaganda." The documents indicated German agents had placed "fire bombs" with delayed timers aboard U.S. ships leaving for Allied ports; tried to sabotage work or cause workers to strike at plants producing munitions for the Allies; blown up munition dumps; and even tried to buy up all supplies of liquid chlorine, which was used for poison gas. One of those implicated was George Viereck, editor of the *Fatherland*, New York's German-American newspaper. His involvement hurt the cause of other German-American publications that were not doing anything wrong.

As feelings of "100 percent Americanism" spread and created bitter reactions against immigrants, the long-dormant Ku Klux Klan (KKK) was being revived in Georgia. The Klan, formed after the Civil War, is a secret society that

A new member takes an oath of allegiance at a Ku Klux Klan meeting in Georgia in 1921. KKK members, who wore hoods and white robes to hide their identities, were racists who pretended to be patriots and preached white supremacy. They committed acts of violence and terror against immigrants, African-Americans, Jews, Roman Catholics, and others they hated simply because they were different.

advocates white supremacy. Now, as feelings about the Great War heated up, the Klan won official recognition from Georgia state government officials. In a rally on Stone Mountain near Atlanta, under a burning cross, Imperial Wizard William Joseph Simmons issued a warning to Americans whom the KKK did not like. He declared it was the Klan's business to make sure that the "self-centered Hebrew, the cultured Greek, the virile Roman and the mystic Oriental" would all "yield" to the Anglo-Saxon. The KKK also maintained its long-standing dislike of African-Americans and Roman Catholics. Simmons's speech was intended to warn some of the newer Americans to watch their step.

Overall, 1915 was a landmark year for the KKK, which also saw its image upgraded in a movie called *Birth of a Nation*. The movie's story line came from a novel called *The Clansman*. The book — dedicated to the KKK — depicted the post-Civil War Reconstruction era as a reign of terror conducted by African-Americans and "Yankees" who came from the victorious North to force their ways on the defeated South. The white-robed KKK members were the heroes, coming out at night to save innocent, white southerners from being brutalized. The movie was the hit of the year across the country and, despite its racist content, is considered a classic in the development of motion pictures. The KKK started anew in 1914 with just a few thousand recruits but by 1924 had an estimated four to five million members throughout the United States.

Also in 1915, a Jew named Leo Frank was lynched in Marietta, Georgia, for allegedly having raped and killed a fourteen-year-old girl named Mary Phagan in 1913. Frank had moved to Georgia from New York, where he had attended Cornell University, to manage a pencil factory owned by his uncle. Phagan worked at the factory, and when she was found murdered, Frank was charged and then convicted after a long trial marred by an outpouring of anti-Semitic hatred. Although the trial was controversial and Frank claimed he was innocent, he was sentenced to death. Outgoing Governor John Stanton had such doubts about Frank's guilt that he commuted the death sentence to life imprisonment. Stanton waited to act until he had only three days left to serve as governor — and then had to leave the state for his own safety. The commutation created an uproar, and three days later a mob stormed the prison where Frank was held. They took him to Marietta, where the girl had lived, and hanged him. The *Journal*, the newspaper in Marietta, absolved the mob: "The people demanded that the verdict of the court [the death sentence] be carried out, and saw to it that it was. We insist they were, and are, law abiding citizens of Georgia."

Lynching, mostly of African-Americans, was a common practice in the South during that period. Tuskegee Institute, an African-American school, kept a yearly record of lynchings. In 1915 there were 69. Although that number was greatly reduced from the 115 lynchings recorded in 1900 and the 130 in 1901, the climate of racial and ethnic antagonism in the United States was stronger than ever. And it was a climate that would bring further fear and suffering to Blacks, immigrants, and other people outside the mainstream of white, Christian, Anglo-Saxon America.

Although many believed Leo Frank was innocent, he was convicted of raping and killing a fourteen-year-old girl in 1913. After his sentence was commuted to life in prison, Frank, who was Jewish, was hanged by a lynch mob in Marietta, Georgia, in 1915.

Lynchings like the one shown here were a common form of mob terror during the early twentieth century, particularly in the rural South, where African-Americans were often singled out for vigilante "justice" by white mobs.

The Great War gave U.S. women new employment opportunities. Many began working in factories that produced ammunition and other war material. Although they were not allowed to engage in combat, many women took part in the war overseas as members of the military or service groups.

CHAPTER THREE

The War Changes America — 1916

When American novelist Mary Roberts Rinehart arrived in Europe as one of the first U.S. writers to cover the Great War, she was given star treatment. Belgian government officials were so eager to have Americans learn about the brutal invasion of their country that they even assigned her an officer and staff car so she could travel back and forth to the Western Front. She obtained exclusive stories for the *Saturday Evening Post* and was the only woman among a group of war correspondents allowed to make a special visit to "no man's land," the area between Allied and Central Powers lines. "This was the first official trip into no man's land allowed to any correspondents by the Allies, and as the men represented many newspapers . . . the story was widely reported," Rinehart reminisced years later. "But I have yet to learn that any one of them reported that a woman accompanied them."

American women played a major role in the Great War. But just as Rinehart was left out of stories written by male correspondents, the accomplishments of U.S. women in the war have also been overlooked by historians. In the United States, the demand for war material created so many new jobs in 1915 and 1916 that more women went to work than ever before. And when the United States joined the fighting in 1917, even more women were called upon to fill positions left vacant by departing soldiers. Also, an estimated twenty-five thousand U.S. women served overseas during the war, some in the U.S. military and many more in service organizations like the Red Cross and YWCA. Nearly 350 American women died overseas during the war, even though women were not allowed to engage in combat as they are today. Women were usually denied permission to work at the front, even as nurses, but it is believed at least one woman was killed at the front during an artillery barrage.

In addition to Rinehart, many American women traveled to Europe before the males of the American Expeditionary Force (the name given to U.S. forces that fought in the war) even started training in 1917. American women volunteered for duty with more than fifty U.S. and forty-five foreign service agencies and war organizations. One such volunteer, Mary Dexter, an ambulance driver with a British unit attached to the French Army, gloried in the exploits

Members of the Red Cross Brigade line up in front of an ambulance. Many American women volunteered in U.S. and foreign service organizations, with some of them going overseas even before the United States entered the war. They worked as nurses, drove ambulances, and performed many other duties vital to the war effort.

of other women. "There are heaps of women driving for the English Army, and for the French — an American spoke to me in the street yesterday who has been chauffing for the French near Amiens for months," she wrote in a letter during the war. (The French word for a woman driver, whether the vehicle she drove was an ambulance, auto, or truck, was *chaufess*.)

Many women who volunteered to work in the war effort came from backgrounds of wealth and affluence. Several women's colleges formed their own service units, including Smith College. Harriet Boyd Hawes, for example, was an 1892 Smith graduate who had served as a nurse in the Greco-Turkish and Spanish-American wars. In 1914, she began doing relief work with the Serbian army. She also led a group of seventeen Smith graduates who went to France in 1917 to assist in the war effort. Each of the volunteers contributed three hundred dollars to pay for a uniform and other equipment, with many continuing to give fifty-five dollars a month so they could stay in Europe and do relief work.

Stalemate

By 1916, the war in which so many American women were already involved was dragging on. The Western Front changed little despite two major offensives, one by the Germans aimed at the French city of Verdun and another by the British at the Somme River. Germany struck first in January when it tried for a breakthrough at Verdun, site of the strongest fortress on the front and a key to Allied strength. The French rallied around the cry of *"On ne passe pas!"* (They shall not pass!) and, with help from other Allied Forces, allowed only small gains by the Germans. The fighting at Verdun raged the entire year, taking the lives of 900,000 French and German soldiers. On July 1, the British, fortified with fresh troops from home, mounted an attack against the Germans at the Somme River. But it was the same old story of the Great War: small gains at a terrific sacrifice of life. On the first day of the battle, more than 50,000 British soldiers were killed — the highest one-day loss of life ever for the British. A total of 1,250,000 British, French, and Germans were killed from July 1 to November 19 in the Battle of the Somme.

The Russians, hoping to ease pressure on the Western Front, attacked strongly in March on the Eastern Front. In June, Russia made its last great effort of the war. In the Brusilov Offensive, the Russians routed the Austrian Army over a two hundred-mile front and advanced deep into Central Powers territory in Austria-Hungary. The push continued through September, with the Russians capturing a great deal of land and more than two hundred thousand prisoners. But counting fatalities, casualties, deserters, and soldiers captured by the enemy, the offensive depleted the Russian Army by about one million men. This led to a breakdown in morale from which the Russians never recovered. Romania joined the war in August on the side of the Allies. But the Central Powers quickly invaded Romania and by December had routed the Romanian Army, remnants of which fled and later joined Russian troops. The victory in Romania was important for the Central Powers because it gave them access to valuable sources of oil and wheat, both badly needed in the war effort.

The Battle of Jutland, the only major sea confrontation of the war, occurred when Germany's High Seas Fleet fought Great Britain's Grand Fleet off the coast of Norway. The two fleets met in force on May 31, 1916. Ships from both sides fought furiously for hours before the surviving German vessels were finally able to slip away. Afterward, both sides claimed victory. However, for the rest of the war, the German fleet never again challenged British supremacy on the open seas. The dreaded German U-boats, however, continued to play a major part in the war by sinking ships that were bringing supplies to the Allies from the United States and other countries.

Technological advancements in the Great War created new weapons that not only killed more efficiently and in new ways but also brought new terror to the battlefield. One of these new horrors of war was the tank. The British, whose tanks were mounted on caterpillar treads, had designed their tanks in secret, hoping their new weapon could crush the Germans. The first forty-two tanks built were rushed into battle in 1916 in the Battle of the Somme, but there were too few of them to have a major impact on the fighting. As with other new technologies, it took time to learn to use them properly. Military leaders eventually realized they needed large numbers of tanks before they

How tanks got their name

Although tanks were frightening to face on the battlefield, the way they got their name is comical. The tank was developed in secret in England at the beginning of the Great War. In 1916, when field tests of the new vehicle began in the English countryside, British officials were worried that citizens would become suspicious of the large, canvas-shrouded prototypes clanking around.

In an effort to conceal the type of vehicle being tested, one official suggested calling it a *water carrier*. He said citizens could be told this strange new vehicle was intended for use in the desert.

But because initials were commonly used during the war for brevity, one planner said he would "not stand for being on anything called the W.C. Committee." *W.C.*, in addition to standing for *water carrier*, are also the initials for water closet, an old-fashioned term for a toilet. To pacify the planner's British sense of taste, the undercover name became *water tank*. And thus the name *tank* was born.

would be truly effective in battle. Nonetheless, the tanks were frightening to the foot soldiers. In those days, even automobiles were a novelty, so a motorized weapon of war astounded them. As the tanks rumbled toward them, the soldiers tried to stop them by firing their rifles, but with no effect. The tanks seemed invincible.

It was not until the Battle of Cambrai in France on November 20, 1917, that tanks came into their own. The British sent 324 tanks crashing into the heavily fortified Hindenburg Line. The tanks rolled through the defenses and, with the foot soldiers who followed close behind, shattered two German divisions and took eight thousand prisoners. In *All Quiet on the Western Front*, by German author Erich Maria Remarque, a soldier comments late in the war that tanks "have become a terrible weapon; more than anything else they embody for us the horror of war."

Profiting from War

The Great War, while creating devastation throughout Europe, was great for the U.S. economy. The U.S. government had pledged neutrality, but its bankers, farmers, and industrial leaders were still free to do business with both the Allies and the Central Powers. From the start, however, U.S. business interests favored the Allies. The first U.S. loan to the Allies was for the relatively small sum of 10 million dollars, but in 1916, a bank consortium headed by financier J. P. Morgan put together another 500 million dollars. By April 1917, shortly before the United States entered the war, Americans had invested a total of more than 2 billion dollars in Allied war bonds, a type of loan, compared to only 2 million dollars in German bonds. Those figures are an accurate gauge of the sentiments of the nation during the U.S. period of official "neutrality."

War was also good for farmers. Even before the United States went to war itself, the war in Europe and the possibility of U.S. involvement had pushed wheat and cotton prices to unprecedented levels. U.S. trade figures for the fiscal year (an accounting period of twelve months) ending in June 1917 showed imports of 2.7 billion dollars and exports of nearly 6.3 billion dollars, an increase in goods leaving the country of more than 35 percent from the previous year. The Allies were buying munitions, weapons, uniforms, food, and just about everything else imaginable. And the war kept using up the material, which meant even more sales. Social commentator William Allen White wrote that war had created "its own intoxication, a kind of economic inflation that had spiritual reflexes. People felt happy because they were busy and seemed to be making money."

Secretary of War Newton D. Baker in a 1915 photograph. A member of President Wilson's cabinet, Baker was in charge of coordinating the U.S. war effort.

Secretary of War Newton Baker said the real might of America was its industry, because war is "the conflict of smokestacks now, the combat of the driving wheel and the engine." But to keep that "driving wheel" turning required labor. The United States had come to depend on immigration to provide a steady supply of new, cheap labor, but the Great War had cut that to a trickle. The result proved to be a huge benefit for minorities, because workers who had been shunned in the past were suddenly in great demand. The need for new workers was the greatest in agriculture, and this demand had a huge effect on Asians and Mexicans living and working in California, Texas, Arizona, and New Mexico.

California, as it had been for the Chinese, was the main destination of Japanese immigrants, and most of them worked in agriculture. Japanese immigration had not begun until 1869, when the first twenty-seven immigrants from Japan arrived and settled near Sacramento. They arrived just sixteen years after U.S. Navy Commodore Matthew Perry had sailed to Japan seeking trade agreements. It was his visit that helped open up Japan to the outside world. By 1890, about twelve thousand Japanese were living in Hawaii, which would become a U.S. territory in a few years and a state in 1959. About three thousand Japanese-Americans were living in the continental United States. In 1917, when the U.S. finally went to war, Japanese-American farmers were growing almost 90 percent of California's celery, onions, and tomatoes as well

The "Yellow Peril"

"Yellow Peril" is a term for the fear some whites had at the beginning of the twentieth century that too many Asians were immigrating to America and gaining too much power and influence. California, the most popular destination for immigrants from China, Japan, and other Asian countries, was a center for these negative racial feelings .

By the time of the Great War, the white reaction to the "Yellow Peril" had forced restrictions on immigration from China and Japan. And Asians who had already immigrated faced a great deal of discrimination in California and other areas where large numbers of them lived.

In 1913, California lawmakers, still responding to cries of "Yellow Peril," passed the Alien Land Act. The law prohibited Asians and other aliens from buying land or leasing it for agricultural purposes for more than three years. However, the act did not have a major effect, because by this time, many children of Asian immigrants had become U.S. citizens and were able to buy and lease land for themselves, their parents, and others.

Also, during the Great War, the demand for agricultural products was so great that local officials did not bother to enforce the law. This resulted in a temporary economic boon for Japanese, Chinese, Koreans, and other Asians who earned their living through growing crops. When the demand for food eased after the war, however, California again began enforcing the restrictions.

as more than 70 percent of its flower products and 35 percent of its grapes. During this time, there were also sizable numbers of Korean and other Asian immigrants making a living in California through farming.

Even before the Great War, large numbers of Mexicans were already employed in Colorado's sugar beet industry, and many others were working in California, Texas, Arizona, and New Mexico. The increased demand for agricultural workers caused by the war sparked a new boom in Mexican immigration. During the war years, it is believed that as many as fifty thousand Mexicans immigrated to the United States legally, with perhaps another one hundred thousand entering illegally. Mexican workers were in such great demand that Congress even exempted them from literacy requirements; Congress also removed the eight-dollar-per-person fee it had approved in the Immigration Act of 1917 for anyone moving to the United States from another country.

The job opportunities for Mexicans were not confined to agriculture, however. The war economy created so many manufacturing jobs that for the first time, Mexicans began moving in sizable numbers to cities in the Northeast and the Midwest. There they worked in steel plants, packing houses, and automobile factories. By the end of the war, some twenty-five hundred Mexicans lived in Detroit and about four thousand in Chicago. Mexican-American communities had also been established in cities such as St. Louis and Kansas City. After the war, however, there were still only about seventy thousand Mexicans living east of the Mississippi River, compared to an estimated seven hundred thousand in Texas, New Mexico, Arizona, and California.

Mexican workers pick strawberries in the Salinas, California, area. During the Great War, thousands of Mexicans came to the United States to work in agriculture and in other areas of the booming war economy. For many, this lowly form of "stoop labor" was a stepping stone to better jobs and a new life in the States.

The greatest societal shift caused by the booming war economy was the mass migration of African-Americans from the South. In 1912, the South was home to 90 percent of African-Americans, most of them working as small tenant farmers or servants. The late 1890s and the first years of the twentieth century had seen the worst violence and the most degrading conditions for Black Americans since Civil War days. In 1893, for example, there were 155 lynchings, and there were 130 in 1901. Southern states had all enacted "Jim Crow" laws, which officially segregated African-Americans by denying them access to restaurants, motels, schools, and other facilities only whites could use. The name for this type of discriminatory legislation came from a nineteenth-century song called "Jump, Jim Crow." The name implied, in a derogatory sense, that the laws were meant to make African-Americans "jump" to the commands of whites.

But by 1916, the war was creating many new jobs in the North. The lure of work and the chance to escape such intolerable social conditions gave birth to a "northern fever" that spread throughout African-Americans living in the South. The result was that more than 550,000 moved north during the war years, with another 900,000 following in the next decade. New York and Chicago were among the main destinations of this flood of people hopeful for a better life. By the end of the war, the Harlem section of New York City had become the largest urban center of people of African descent in the world. The north-

This ramshackle home is typical of the miserable living conditions that many African-Americans had to endure in the South at the turn of the century. During the Great War, more than one-half million African-Americans moved to northern cities in search of a better life. They sought to escape violence, grinding poverty, and the lack of freedom caused by racism.

ern migration, although slowed during the years of the Great Depression, continued through World War II and made African-Americans a predominantly urban group.

As labor agents moved from town to town in the South recruiting African-American and other workers for factories and other businesses, people left by the thousands. Some small communities became African-American ghost towns, especially those where their treatment by whites had been especially brutal. One woman in a Mississippi town that had lost half of its African-Americans to "northern fever" said she would "go wild" if she had to stay there any longer. "Every time I go home I have to pass house after house of all my friends who are in the North and are prospering," she said. Gradually, southern whites woke up to the fact that their traditional source of cheap labor was fleeing. The *Tifton Gazette* in Georgia said African-Americans were leaving because whites had "allowed Negroes to be lynched, five at a time, on nothing stronger than suspicion . . . they have allowed them to be . . . whipped, and their homes burned. . . . Loss of much of the State's best labor is one of the prices Georgia is paying for unchecked mob activity against Negroes often charged only with ordinary crimes."

The move north was not always good for African-Americans. They ran into more hatred, and major race riots hit many northern cities during the war years. African-Americans often had trouble adjusting to new climates and cultures, and their working conditions and pay were not always adequate. But in general, they found better conditions than in the South, where life for most had been sheer misery.

Pancho Villa and his wife in Juarez, Mexico, in 1914. Although he was branded a criminal by U.S. officials, many people in Mexico looked up to him as a revolutionary who was fighting a corrupt Mexican government. Villa opposed the United States because he felt its policies oppressed Mexicans.

U.S. Military Activities South of the Border
Although still reluctant to go to war in Europe, the United States in 1916 did not mind using its military might in Mexico and Santo Domingo (now known as the Dominican Republic). And the previous year, the United States had sent its forces into Haiti (a move that would be duplicated in 1994 when the United States intervened in Haiti to help President Jean-Bertrand Aristide regain power). The United States' biggest military activity in 1916 was conducted against Pancho Villa. Although he considered himself a revolutionary general, Villa was branded a bandit by both the United States and Mexico. For example, he once set up a slaughterhouse on the U.S.-Mexican border and sold stolen beef to American meatpackers. He opposed the Mexican government led by President Venustiano Carranza and battled the United States. He felt the United States oppressed Mexicans and had interfered in Mexican affairs by helping Carranza win political control. He raided back and forth across the border through early 1916.

On March 9, Villa led a force of about fifteen hundred in a raid on Columbus, New Mexico, that resulted in the deaths of seventeen Americans. U.S. troops pursued, killing fifty of Villa's men before they got across the border and another seventy after crossing over into Mexico. The U.S. government decided it had to stop Villa, and President Woodrow Wilson dispatched Brigadier General John J. "Black Jack" Pershing across the border into Mexico. The military expedition by Pershing and a force of fifteen thousand was not very successful, as they failed to catch Villa. "Black Jack" went on to greater glory as the leader of the American Expeditionary Force that went to Europe to fight in the Great War.

In May, the United States dispatched troops to Santo Domingo to settle internal violence in that Caribbean nation. The problems were both financial and political. The United States set up an internal administration that ruled the country until 1924, when the naval officers who were in charge finally left the country. In 1915, the United States had also intervened in Haiti to protect U.S. investments in that country's national bank and railroad. The military occupation made the country a U.S. protectorate for many years. In August 1916, the United States extended its influence in the Caribbean by signing a treaty with Denmark to buy the Danish West Indies for twenty-five million dollars. One factor that led to the purchase of the Virgin Islands (their new U.S. name) was the fear that Germany wanted them as a naval base.

In this 1915 photograph taken at the International Bridge at El Paso, Texas, Pancho Villa (center) stands between two men who later became his enemies: Mexican General Alvaro Obregon (left) and U.S. General John J. "Black Jack" Pershing (right). Obregon, who later became president of Mexico, opposed Villa politically. Pershing two years later would unsuccessfully lead an army into Mexico to try and capture Villa.

Hawaii comes under U.S. influence

In the early years of the twentieth century, when the U.S. military intervened in several foreign countries, the reason was often the need to protect U.S. business interests. The United States usually did not take over the countries it invaded, but in one case it did. In fact, that is how the sun-kissed islands of Hawaii, which are separated from the U.S. mainland by several thousand miles, became the fiftieth U.S. state.

In 1893, American businessman Sanford B. Dole, who was doing business in Hawaii, established a revolutionary "committee of safety" whose purpose was to topple Queen Liliuokalani (pictured here), who headed the Hawaiian monarchy. The committee was made up of businessmen who resented the queen's interference in their affairs. Dole gained support for the overthrow of the Hawaiian monarch from John L. Stevens, the U.S. minister to Hawaii.

On January 16, 1893, Stevens ordered U.S. Marines from the cruiser *Boston* to protect U.S. life and property, even though there was no real threat to any U.S. business ventures or citizens. Queen Liliuokalani was imprisoned in her own palace, which today is a major historical attraction in Honolulu.

President Grover Cleveland felt Queen Liliuokalani had been illegally overthrown and refused to annex Hawaii. But when the Spanish-American War in 1898 proved Hawaii's military value as a naval base, its fate was sealed. In 1900, it was annexed as a territory, and in 1959, it became the fiftieth state.

In 1853, the first official Hawaii census reported 71,019 native Hawaiians, less than one-quarter of the number who had lived there before Europeans started arriving in the late 1700s. Like other Pacific Islanders, Hawaiians were susceptible to infectious diseases carried by Europeans and Americans, and tens of thousands had died from such diseases as measles and smallpox. By 1910, the native Hawaiian population had fallen to only 38,547, just 24.7 percent of Hawaii's total. Although the actual number of Hawaiians and Hawaiians of mixed ancestry has increased rapidly since then, their percentage of the total population in Hawaii has continued to decline.

Hawaiians today are, sadly, a minority in the land they once ruled. Like Native Americans on the mainland, the Hawaiians are waging a battle to regain some of the sovereignty that they once enjoyed over their own affairs.

Election of 1916

The divisions over the Great War continued in the United States in 1916, and the argument over whether the nation should join the war was played out in the presidential elections. Former President Theodore Roosevelt still led the group that thought the United States should join the Allies, and he was merciless in his criticism of President Wilson. Wilson, who had won his first term in 1912, was nominated by the Democrats and ran against Republican Charles Hughes. The campaign slogan for the Democrats was "He kept us out of war!" But Wilson was not entirely comfortable with that phrase. By 1916, he had already swung over to the side of those backing U.S. military preparedness, and his pro-Allied sentiments were starting to get the best of him.

Wilson won the popular vote 9.1 million to 8.5 million, but the election was much closer than those figures indicate. The Electoral College score — the tally of votes apportioned to each state on the basis of population — is what really elects a president. In that key balloting, Wilson got 277 votes to 254 for Hughes. The election was so close that the outcome was not known until three days after the election, when it was finally determined that Wilson had won California by just 3,773 votes. That state's thirteen electoral votes gave him his margin of victory.

The irony of the 1916 election is that five months after Wilson's victory, the man who kept Americans out of war got them into it.

President Woodrow Wilson working at his desk in the White House in 1917. He failed to keep the United States out of the Great War, and he failed again in trying to work out a just peace once the fighting had ended.

I WANT YOU
FOR U.S. ARMY
NEAREST RECRUITING STATION

This poster by James Montgomery Flagg calls on Americans to fight for their country. It is probably the most famous portrayal ever of the mythical Uncle Sam, who is supposed to represent the spirit of U.S. patriotism. Posters such as this were part of the propaganda effort to make Americans back U.S. involvement in the war.

CHAPTER FOUR

America Goes to War — 1917

Although Americans had been divided about the war since 1914, the sentiments of the president and most citizens had gradually shifted toward the Allies. Thus, in 1917, it did not take much to push the United States into entering the Great War. Three key incidents led to this momentous decision.

On February 1, Germany announced resumption of unrestricted submarine warfare. Wilson responded by severing diplomatic relations with Germany.

On February 24, Great Britain gave U.S. officials a copy of a note German Foreign Secretary Arthur Zimmermann had sent in January to Germany's foreign office in Mexico. The British had intercepted and decoded what became known as the "Zimmermann message." In it, the Germans asked Mexico to go to war against the United States if it joined the Allies. Germany even promised to help Mexico win back the parts of New Mexico, Texas, and Arizona that the United States had taken away from Mexico in the past. On February 28, Wilson made the message public, and it further inflamed the passion for war that was already gaining strength in the United States. An unfortunate side effect of the "Zimmermann message," however, was that Mexican-Americans, especially those living in southwestern states like Texas, were now considered possible enemies. In the past, Mexican-Americans had often been targets of racism. Now such incidents increased in number and became more violent.

On March 16, it was reported that three U.S. ships, the *City of Memphis*, the *Illinois*, and the *Valencia*, had been sunk by U-boats. This pushed President Wilson to finally make the decision he had long dreaded — to go to war. Five days later, he ordered a special session of Congress. On April 2, in an eloquent, impassioned speech that is one of the most famous ever given by a president, Wilson asked Congress to declare war. "The world must be made safe for democracy," said Wilson.

His speech included all-out appeals to patriotism and fighting words to rally America's battle spirit. But Wilson also invited other nations to help the United States create a new world order after the war. The president envisioned a new society that would "rise from the wreckage of a Europe torn asunder by

The U.S. propaganda campaign

The Great War saw the advent of many new weapons to conquer the body, from tanks to tear gas. But perhaps even more powerful was one to conquer the mind — propaganda.

When the war started, the Allied and Central Powers had both used propaganda to try to sway the United States to their side. Now that the United States had joined the war, the nation itself constructed the most imposing propaganda machine the world had ever seen. George Creel, a former newspaper and magazine writer who headed the Committee of Public Information, saw his job as "a vast enterprise in salesmanship, the world's greatest adventure in advertising." His task was to convince Americans and the entire world of the rightness of the U.S. war effort.

At first, the committee only helped reporters get information for their stories. But Creel began to mobilize the nation's artists to draw posters, pictures, and other works with patriotic themes. The committee's Division of Pictorial Publicity included famous artists like Montgomery Flagg, who created the legendary "Uncle Sam Wants You" Army recruiting poster. Creel also enlisted the new motion picture industry, which churned out patriotic films like *Pershing's Crusader* and lined up stars like Douglas Fairbanks for rallies to help sell war bonds.

Creel flooded the nation with patriotic literature. His committee printed 6.8 million copies of one pamphlet called "How the War Came to America," including more than one million copies in Swedish, Polish, Italian, Spanish, and other foreign languages. The committee even wrote leaflets to induce enemy soldiers to lay down their arms (they were delivered in artillery shells that did not explode), supplied news stories about the U.S. war effort to every nation (including some three hundred newspapers in China), and worked in many other ways to influence world opinion.

The spoken word was also a big part of this patriotic campaign. Creel organized about 75,000 "four-minute men" to give patriotic speeches. They appeared at schools, churches, war bond rallies, and many other public and private meetings across the nation. It is estimated more than 314 million people heard them deliver some 7.5 million patriotic messages.

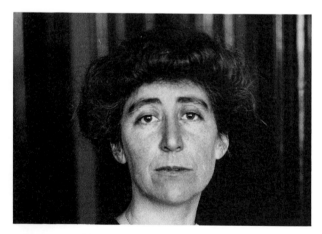

Jeannette Rankin, who in 1917 became the first female member of the House of Representatives, voted "no" on a declaration of war against Germany. Ironically, she was also a member of Congress in 1941 and voted "no" again on whether the United States should enter World War II.

the evil spirits of imperial plunder and dynastic rivalries; so subject peoples, long suppressed and exploited, might recover the precious independence that Americans had enjoyed since the founding of their nation." He said all nations should band together to work for peace, and he also promised "the liberation of [all] peoples." Those words especially were welcomed by people living in countries dominated by other nations. His speech was reported around the world and helped spur the rising tide of nationalism that became one of the legacies of the Great War.

On April 4, the Senate voted for war by a vote of 82 to 6, and the House concurred two days later, 373 to 50. One of those voting against war was Congresswoman Jeannette Rankin, a Montana Republican who on that day also made history by being sworn in as the first female member of the House. It was a difficult vote, and Rankin, who opposed war, passed on the first roll call. On the second roll call, she stood up and said, her voice breaking with emotion, "I want to stand by my country, but I cannot vote for war." Rankin served one term, from 1917 to 1919, but, in one of the strange ironies of American history, was elected again in 1941. She voted "no" again on December 8, 1941, when President Franklin Delano Roosevelt

asked Congress for a declaration of war against Japan. His plea came one day after the Japanese had attacked Pearl Harbor in Hawaii.

The "Melting Pot" Troops

Just as the United States itself was considered a racial, religious, and ethnic "melting pot," the American Expeditionary Force (AEF) it sent to fight in the war was a mixture of various races and ethnic groups. There were many soldiers whose parents had come from foreign lands, such as Mexico, Germany, Italy, Austria, Poland, China, Britain, and Russia. Sometimes the soldiers themselves were born abroad and immigrated to the United States. New York City had been the gateway to America for millions of immigrants, many of whom settled in that huge city. So it was not surprising that the Seventy-seventh Division's New Yorkers contained soldiers of many nationalities. In fact, it was nicknamed the "Melting Pot Division." The soldiers of the Seventy-seventh could speak a combined total of forty-two languages, and among its numbers were Jewish, Chinese, Russian, Italian, German, Turkish, and Greek immigrants. Their shoulder patch was a white Statue of Liberty on a blue shield trimmed in red.

Sergeant Sing Kee, a Chinese-American, became one of the heroes of the Seventy-seventh Kee was among the thirty men operating a message center in the village of Monte Notre Dame during the Third Battle of the Aisne in June 1918. When all twenty-nine of his fellow operators were killed in shelling from enemy guns, Sing remained at his post alone for twenty-four hours. Despite the horror of having seen so many of his comrades killed, Sing continued sending vital messages throughout the battle.

These U.S. soldiers training for war carried wooden sticks instead of rifles as they marched. It took months to train men and get them the equipment they needed before they could be sent to fight overseas. As they marched, the soldiers might have sung "Over There," a popular tune about how Americans were going to Europe to win the war.

American Indians fight for citizenship

One of the great ironies of the Great War is that Native Americans fought to defend a government that had taken their land and nearly destroyed their culture. But in the process, they went a long way toward winning their battle to become U.S. citizens.

Before the Great War, most American Indians lived on reservations and were denied U.S. citizenship. This meant they were denied many rights, such as being able to vote. But when the United States went to war, some seventeen thousand Native Americans served in the armed forces. And they fought well, with 10 earning the coveted Croix de Guerre and another 150 winning other medals for bravery. One of the greatest single feats of the war was accomplished by Joseph Oklahombie, a Choctaw. He singlehandedly overran several German machine gun nests and captured more than one hundred enemy soldiers.

The Second Division, which in 1918 fought in the battle of Blanc Mont from September 26 to October 13, had units from Texas and Oklahoma that included Cherokees and Apaches. Some units in the 2nd Division had little fear of their radio messages being intercepted by the enemy; they talked in Native languages that mystified any Germans who might hear them. (Navajo code-talkers did the same thing in World War II.)

Cato Sells, the U.S. commissioner of Indian affairs, led the fight after the war to have Congress grant citizenship to Indian military veterans. He argued that they had fought in integrated regiments "side by side with the white man, not as Indians, but as Americans." Congress agreed and in 1919 granted citizenship to Native veterans. That was only the first step, but a major one, in the effort to have American Indians recognized as citizens. That finally happened in 1924 with the passage of the Indian Citizen Act.

The fame of American Indian soldiers was widespread, both during and after the war. In 1925, Hollywood even made a film called *The Vanishing American*. It is the story of a Navajo who fights valiantly in World War I and then returns to his reservation, only to have to deal with a crooked official on the reservation. In an era when prejudice was rising, the filmmakers took a risk by casting a Native American as the hero. The film was evidence of the positive impact the war service of Indians had created in the minds of other Americans.

Soldiers from many different nations fought on the Western Front. The battlefield often became a crazy quilt of ethnic groups, with a confusing mixture of different languages rising at times above the roar of the chattering machine guns and exploding artillery shells. In August 1918, Sergeant Metej Kocak, a Hungarian-American immigrant who had been a coal miner before the war, was fighting with the Fifth Marine Regiment of the Second Division near Soissons, a French town. When his division's advance was stopped by a German machine gunner, Kocak made his way forward alone. Singlehandedly, he routed a squad of German infantry, saving his platoon. As the fighting continued, he became separated from the U.S. forces and encountered a group of soldiers from Senegal, a French colony in Africa. Their officer had been killed. Kocak took command of the Africans. Fighting together, Kocak and the troops from Senegal captured two more machine gun positions before the day was over.

The Moroccan Division of the French Army, manned by North African Muslims, also fought side by side with U.S. troops in that battle. General James Harbord, who was commanding the Second Division, called the Moroccans "the best shock and assault troops in France." Soldiers found out that in the heat of battle, race and nationality do not matter very much.

For most soldiers, the ethnic diversity they encountered in the service was a new experience. Back home in the United States, they had usually lived and worked with people of similar backgrounds, heritage, and views. But the war brought the soldiers in close contact with people from other races and nationalities. Many journalists focused on this multicultural aspect of the war in stories they wrote for U.S. newspapers. One such story quoted an Irish-American soldier praising a Chinese-American who had manned a machine gun: "You oughter see that Chink talking Mongolian to a machine gun, and believe me he sure made it understand him. I'm here to say that when a Chink fights, he's a fighting son-of-a-gun and don't let anybody kid you different." Although the term used to refer to the Chinese-American is itself derogatory, the Irish-American soldier was honoring his counterpart for his fighting ability — and on the field of battle, there is no praise greater than that. The war made some soldiers realize that even if other people did not look like them or have the same background, they could still be admired.

More than 200,000 Black American soldiers went overseas with the AEF, and more than 367,000 African-Americans in all served in the military during the Great War. There were so many African-American soldiers that in 1917, Secretary of War Newton Baker appointed Emmett J. Scott, former secretary to famed African-American educator Booker T. Washington, as a special assistant on military race relations. One obstacle Scott could not overcome was that African-Americans were segregated during the war. They served in all-Black units that were usually commanded by white officers. Although this was a continuation of the segregation they faced at home, it did not stop African-Americans from fighting bravely.

One of the biggest heroes of the war was Private (later Sergeant) Henry Johnson of Albany, New York. A porter who back home had loaded luggage for the New York Central Railroad, Johnson was a member of the 369th Regiment, the one that had been rushed to war to avoid a race riot in Spartanburg, South Carolina. On the night of May 11, 1918, Johnson was positioned in a forward observation post with Needham Roberts of Trenton, New Jersey, when more than twenty German soldiers attacked. A grenade wounded Roberts, but Johnson fought on alone, even after being shot several times himself and wound-

Henry Johnson, wearing his medal from the French government, has a huge smile as he arrives home after the war. A railroad porter in Albany, New York, Johnson was one of the United States' greatest heroes in the Great War. His regiment, the 369th, was the most decorated African-American unit in the war.

ed by a grenade. When he ran out of bullets, he used his rifle like a club. Then, he started slashing with a bolo knife, a weapon weighing several pounds with a blade nine inches long. He also rescued Roberts when the Germans tried to carry him away as a prisoner. As the Germans finally fled in panic, Johnson lobbed grenades after them. In the skirmish, Johnson killed a total of five enemy soldiers. A few days later, New York City newspapers ran his story under a banner headline, "The Battle of Henry Johnson." He and his fellow soldiers in the 369th, who had been outcasts in Spartanburg, were honored across the country. "Our colored volunteers from Harlem," one reporter wrote, "had become, in a day, one of the famous fighting regiments of the World War."

For his valor, Johnson became the first U.S. soldier to receive the Croix de Guerre (War Cross), France's highest military honor. The 369th as a unit also won that coveted medal for the long, bloody days they spent helping to win France's freedom from Germany. The unit was under fire for a total of 191 days in the Great War, and fifteen hundred men were killed or wounded. Major Arthur Little, who after the war wrote a book about their experiences called *From Harlem to the Rhine*, said the unit's soldiers were welcomed as liberators. "France had kissed their colored soldiers — kissed them with reverence and in honor, first upon the right cheek and then the left," he said, referring to the French tradition of kissing soldiers on each cheek when awarding them medals.

These were some of the first female members of the U.S. Marines. The Great War was the first in which the United States recruited a significant number of women to serve in its armed forces.

Another ingredient in the military melting pot was women. The Great War was the first in which the U.S. military employed large numbers of women, although not all of them served overseas. Army and navy enlistments for the Nurse Corps topped ten thousand, and the navy recruited thirteen thousand women as clerks. They were known as "yeomanettes," a variation of the navy term "yeoman," or a naval officer who performs clerical duties. Even the marines signed up more than three hundred women. The Army Signal Corps organized thirty-three bilingual U.S. women to operate its telephone system in France. They earned two nicknames for their valuable service: "soldiers of the switchboard" and the more popular "hello girls." The Women's Army Motor Corps was formed to allow women to handle driving duties to free men for the battlefields. The women delivered hospital supplies, drove doctors to hospital sites, transported patients, and handled a wide variety of transportation duties for civilian hospitals.

A nurse for the Red Cross watches in 1918 as a soldier from Senegal, a French colony in Africa, uses his artificial limbs to write a letter thanking the American Red Cross for caring for him. He lost both his arms in the Great War while fighting on behalf of France.

Black women in the war

A few African-American women were allowed to go to Europe during the Great War. Their mission was to make life more tolerable for the more than two hundred thousand African-American soldiers who served there. Four of them, sponsored by the Young Men's Christian Association (YMCA), worked in canteens and other hospitality facilities. This group included Addie Hunton and Kathryn Johnson, who wrote a book after the war entitled *Two Colored Women with the American Expeditionary Forces*. Like most women volunteers, they were kept far from the actual front. For the most part, they worked with African-American soldiers who worked as dock workers, engineers, and common laborers.

In their book, Hunton and Johnson recalled that the war brought them "the greatest opportunity for service we had ever known." Working in military canteens, they created reading and reception rooms for African-American soldiers. They made themselves available to talk about music, art, and religion with soldiers, who ranged from graduates of colleges such as Howard, Morehouse, and Clark, to those who were illiterate. Hunton and Johnson taught some of the latter how to write their names. During the outbreak of influenza that devastated U.S. forces in 1918, they nursed soldiers, white as well as African-American.

Hunton and Johnson discovered prejudice against African-American troops by both officers and common soldiers. They told of a young college student who had thought the war would be an opportunity to break away from the racism at home. He came to Europe a sergeant, but a white company commander came to resent him. A "series of humiliations began" that ended with the soldier losing his rank and being locked up in the guardhouse. "His face hurt us as often as we looked upon it, so full it was of the endurance of an outraged manhood," they wrote.

African-American soldiers were much better accepted by the the people they had come to liberate from the Germans. "The colored soldiers were greatly loved by the French people," Hunton and Johnson wrote. "While passing through the town of Laon, which had been in the hands of the Germans for four years, the French civilians knelt by the roadside and kissed the hands of the 370th infantry, so grateful were they for their deliverance."

Julia C. Stimson was an Army head nurse. In a letter home, she voiced the excitement women felt about this unique (at the time) opportunity to serve their country. She wrote, "To be in the first group of women ever called out for duty with the United States Army, and in the first part of the Army ever sent off on an expeditionary affair of this kind, is all too much good fortune for any one person."

Special Challenges for African-American Soldiers

The 369th Regiment, the most decorated African-American unit in the Great War, was also one of the first shipped overseas, arriving in France in November of 1917. And the 369th had Southern racists to thank for that honor. Organized in New York, the regiment was sent to Spartanburg, South Carolina, to finish training in mid-1917. Before the African-American soldiers even arrived, however, the mayor there warned of trouble because of "their Northern ideas about race equality." He was right. However, the problems were caused not by the African-Americans but by white racists who harassed, taunted, and sometimes beat the soldiers when they came into town.

In the climactic incident, Sergeant Noble Sissle, a drum major in the 369th's famed regimental band, entered a hotel to buy a newspaper for bandleader Lieutenant James Reese Europe. A white civilian beat and kicked Sissle for daring to walk into the segregated hotel, but white soldiers jumped to Sissle's aid. The incident nearly developed into a riot as soldiers and civilians fought. It ended when Europe ordered all the soldiers, black and white, to leave. The U.S. Army's solution to this racial problem was to dispatch the 369th to the war as soon as possible.

African-American officers in 1918 pose with a French girl, whose country they had come to free from the Germans. African-American soldiers fought well in the Great War but were forced to serve in segregated units. Their officers were often whites because the army did not like promoting African-Americans.

Jazz goes to war

When different cultures meet, even during times as dangerous and sad as wartime, they can learn from one another. This happened in the Great War when African-American soldiers brought along a new kind of music that had sprung from their own personal experience, their very own souls. It was called jazz.

Jazz was a uniquely African-American sound developed from ragtime and blues. It had a freedom and musical poetry unlike anything else ever heard before in America. "Memphis Blues," by W. C. Handy, and many other jazz tunes had started to become popular in the United States before the war. When African-American soldiers began playing jazz overseas, Europeans were amazed at the strange new music. But they also liked it, and jazz quickly became popular.

The 369th Regiment from New York had a regimental band famous for its many fine musicians. This crack musical outfit is believed to have been the first to introduce jazz to Europeans. The band debuted jazz in the many concerts it performed in France for soldiers and civilians.

The band's conductor was Lieutenant James Reese Europe, who before the war had conducted orchestras in New York and been a musical director of Broadway plays. The band's drum major was Sergeant Noble Sissle, who later became a singer, conductor, and composer on Broadway.

Sissle and Europe were involved in a fight with white citizens in Spartanburg, South Carolina, that led to their regiment being sent to the Great War ahead of schedule. Their band had also performed in Spartanburg in an attempt to win friends. But they found a much more receptive audience in France than they did in South Carolina.

In the Sissle incident, the Army was acting out of fear of another bloody incident like the one involving the Twenty-fourth Infantry. An African-American unit with a long record of military service, the Twenty-fourth had been stationed in Houston, Texas, to guard a military construction site. White citizens and Houston police officers shouted racial slurs at off-duty soldiers and beat them. Complaints by soldiers failed to stop the racial abuse. On August 23, 1917, Sergeant Vida Henry led a group of about one hundred armed soldiers into town, where they fought with police and civilians in an attempt to get even for the way they had been treated. In the bloody melee that followed, twenty people were killed or injured, most of them white. Punishment was swift, and sixty-three soldiers were indicted for disobeying orders, aggravated assault, mutiny, and murder. All were court martialed, with nineteen sentenced to die by hanging and the others to life imprisonment.

Thus, for African-Americans, military life was not much different from civilian life. In the army, they were still segregated and often worked as laborers, cooks, and mess hall attendants. They discovered that wearing a uniform did not change the way some people treated them. And the fact that they were willing to die for their country did not stop racist actions against the families and friends they had left behind. The northern migration of Black Americans was creating racial tensions, and major race riots erupted in the North during the war. The bloodiest race riot in the twentieth century occurred in July 1917 in East St. Louis, Illinois, when at least thirty-nine African-Americans were killed, many of them burned alive in their own homes. Whites had previously driven cars through the African-American area and shot at houses. When residents saw another car drive by, they fired into it in retaliation. But it was a police car, and two detectives were killed. Whites rioted, destroying African-American homes, killing their occupants, and forcing several hundred more people to flee for their lives.

An African-American man is given an armed escort for protection after a riot in East St. Louis, Illinois, in 1917. Whites attacked African-Americans, killing at least thirty-nine and destroying many of their homes. It is considered to be the worst race riot in the twentieth century.

The reality of life in the United States for African-Americans was so grim that many volunteered when war was declared on April 6, 1917, and the army filled its quota of Blacks in one week. More than two million Blacks registered for the draft, and nearly four hundred thousand served in the military. African-Americans comprised 10 percent of the U.S. population, but they were rarely represented in other jobs by numbers proportionate to their population. Nonetheless, they made up 13 percent of inductees. Part of this was caused by discrimination by draft boards in the South. One draft board in Atlanta inducted 97 percent of registered African-Americans while deferring 85 percent of whites.

It may be difficult to understand why a group that had been denied basic rights in the United States would rush to defend it. Although he hated how his people were treated, civil rights leader W. E. B. Du Bois in 1917 told African-Americans, "[We must] close our ranks shoulder to shoulder with our own white citizens. If this is our country, then this is our war." Du Bois said African-Americans had a chance to show they deserved to be treated with respect and as full citizens. Robert S. Abbott, who owned the *Chicago Defender*, an African-American newspaper, also urged participation. "The colored soldier who fights side by side with the white American in the titanic struggle now ranging across the sea will hardly be begrudged a fair chance when the victorious armies return," he wrote. Despite that, Du Bois and other African-Americans saw the essential injustice of African-Americans fighting for a nation that denied them many rights. On July 28, 1917, about fifteen thousand African-Americans, including Du Bois, marched in New York in The Silent Protest Parade. One banner they carried said, "Mr. President, Why Not Make America Safe for Democracy?" President Woodrow Wilson had used that phrase just a few months earlier in justifying U.S. entry into the Great War; protesters wanted to know why he could not make the United States a safe place for African-Americans.

Fighting in 1917

The United States joined the war at a time when the Allies were exhausted and struggling against the Central Powers. The entry of the United States was decisive in winning the war, not only because of its soldiers but because of the credit it extended to the Allies and the war material it continued to produce. In the last two years of the war, the United States loaned Allied countries seven billion dollars. The funds enabled the Allies to buy supplies from American firms, everything from artillery shells to airplane engines. When it joined the war, the United States asked that it be designated an "Associated" and not an "Allied" power. It wanted to differentiate itself from the original combatants. However, historians generally use the term "Allies" to refer to both the United States and the Allied nations.

Nearly 2 million U.S. soldiers went overseas during the war with the American Expeditionary Force (AEF), and about 1.4 million engaged in combat. The A.E.F. was commanded by General John J. "Black Jack" Pershing, a nickname that referred to his command of African-American cavalry troops in Montana early in his career. Pershing arrived in France in late June 1917 with a small staff. On July 4, a regiment paraded gaily through the streets of Paris. But it took time to train American soldiers, and U.S. forces were not a major factor in fighting until 1918.

The Allies were dealt a severe blow in March 1917 when the Romanov dynasty of Czar Nicholas II was overthrown. The huge Russian army, which had waged a strong fight against the Central Powers on the Eastern Front, was in disarray after the revolution. It kept on fighting but was not very effective. The Bolshevik Revolution in November brought to power the communists, who did not want to continue the war. On December 15, Russia quit fighting against the Central Powers and in 1918 signed a peace treaty called the Treaty of Brest-Litovsk. The Russian withdrawal from the war allowed Germany to concentrate its forces on the Western Front for the final year of the war, 1918.

W. E. B. (William Edward Burghardt) Du Bois was a fiery early leader in the fight for African-American rights. In 1906, Du Bois was one of the founders of the National Association for the Advancement of Colored People. He predicted racial problems for the United States in 1900 when he said that "the problem of the twentieth century is the problem of the color line."

The continuing horror of trench warfare had so demoralized French troops that in late April 1917 a mutiny broke out. Soldiers rebelled when ordered back to the front line. They said, "We'll defend the trenches, but we won't attack." Marshal Henri Petain, the new French commander, decided to appease the soldiers. He adopted a defensive strategy that meant less danger for them. He counseled troops to "wait for the Americans."

Also in 1917, the Italians suffered a stinging defeat at Caporetto, sustaining 500,000 casualties and losing 250 soldiers who were taken prisoner. The Allies' biggest problem, however, was the devastation from unrestricted submarine warfare. The Germans sank 181 ships in January, 259 in February, 325 in March, and 430 in April. The April sinkings alone represented 815,000 gross tons of shipping available to carry war supplies from the United States. In fact, the Germans were sinking ships faster than the Allies could build them. But that changed with U.S. entry into the war. Hundreds of U.S. Navy ships were deployed to the Atlantic, allowing the Allies to set up a transatlantic convoy system to provide protection for merchant ships. The first convoys sailed from the United States in May. They proved so successful that convoys began accompanying ships everywhere in the war area. The armed escorts even began destroying many submarines, and the U-boat threat began to decrease in the second half of 1917.

Loss of Freedom at Home

When Pershing took command of the AEF on May 7, the United States had a small army. Although its navy was powerful, the United States had almost no aircraft, no tanks, and very little in the way of supplies or armaments. Although the conscription, or drafting (forced participation), of soldiers had caused rioting in major cities during the Civil War, the United States decided it required a military draft to raise the huge army it needed. The name *Selective Service* was chosen because officials thought it was less intimidating than the term *conscription*. During the Great War, more than 24 million men registered and more than 2.8 million were drafted.

Nattily dressed young men line up on New York's Lower East Side to register for the draft. Millions of Americans registered and were drafted so the United States could field an army big enough to help win the Great War. Although there were riots when a draft began during the Civil War, there were no problems in 1917.

The United States had to mobilize for war quickly, and in the process, the federal government grew more powerful than ever before. Congress granted President Wilson special wartime powers to organize and direct the country's resources so they could be focused on providing war materials. These included its railroads, steel mills, and other industries. Wilson also created a War Industries Board that was headed by Wall Street financier Bernard Baruch. Baruch gathered together business and industry leaders for advice on decisions about war production. But when it counted, Baruch and the board had the power to command factories or steel mills to do whatever the government wanted. Such central control was unprecedented in a country that prided itself on economic freedom, but the business world obeyed its orders willingly. Industry did not mind the centralized control because the war was very profitable. New businesses were fondly nicknamed "war babies" and their owners "war millionaires."

Future president Herbert Hoover became head of the Food Administration, which directed crop production and distribution. The agency also tried to persuade Americans to curb consumption of wheat, sugar, fat, and meat. Those food items and many more were desperately needed to feed U.S. soldiers, as well as civilian and military populations in Allied countries where food was scarce. The agency ordered wheatless Mondays and Wednesdays, meatless Tuesdays, and porkless Thursdays and Saturdays, that is, days when U.S. citizens were urged not to eat such foods. The Fuel Administration was set up to ration gasoline and coal, which was burned to provide heat for homes.

The United States was a nation born out of a desire by its citizens for personal freedom, but when it entered the war, its citizens were stripped of many of the rights they held so dear. President Wilson and Congress saw a need to crush all dissent and to prevent any sabotage of the war effort. "It is not an army we must shape and train for war. It is a nation," said Wilson. That attitude resulted in passage of the Espionage Act, the Trading With the Enemy Act, and the Sedition Act. All three were designed to protect the war effort by placing limitations on freedom of speech and action. The Espionage Act (June 15, 1917) included the King Amendment, which was aimed at foreign-language newspapers. It required newspapers to give local postmasters English translations of stories before they could be printed. If censors found anything they felt would hurt the war effort, the newspaper could not be mailed.

Herbert Hoover, wearing a high, starched collar, points to bags of flour being shipped to feed the hungry in Europe. Hoover, who became president in 1929, was head of the Food Administration during the war. He was responsible for making sure Europeans caught up in the agony of the Great War, as well as Americans, had enough to eat.

Milwaukee, the largest city in Wisconsin, had both a large German-American population and a strong tradition of socialism, an economic system in which businesses, factories, and farms are owned by the people as a whole and run by the government. The *Milwaukee Leader* was published by Socialists Oscar Ameringer and Victor Berger. When they continued to oppose the war, the postmaster general revoked the newspaper's mailing privileges and refused to deliver mail to the paper. Berger was finally indicted under the Espionage Act and sentenced to prison. While his case was being appealed in 1918, he ran for Congress and was elected — but the House refused to seat him because he opposed the war.

The government also cracked down on African-American newspapers. The editors of *The Messenger* in New York were sentenced to two and one-half years in jail for running a story titled "Pro-Germanism Among Negroes." Randolph Bourne wrote an article in the paper critical of U.S. involvement, saying, "The real enemy is war rather than Imperial Germany."

The federal government used the new laws to punish groups or individuals it felt were criticizing it. This included members of the Women's Party, which was leading the suffrage movement to give women the right to vote in elections. The suffrage movement had been gaining strength for many years, and in 1916 and 1917, women had picketed the White House regularly without much fuss. But after the United States entered the war, their protests were viewed differently because the Women's Party still opposed the war and U.S. involvement in it. The protesters carried banners critical of the U.S. war effort, and these signs came to be considered treasonous. After a major protest at the White House in June 1917, police began arresting women for picketing the White House. During the two years of U.S. participation in the war, about one hundred women were arrested in these protests. Many refused to pay any fines and started hunger strikes while in jail.

The Suffering of German-Americans and Other Immigrants

War creates a mood of us-versus-them that is felt not only on the battlefield but also at home. German-Americans, even those who had lived in the United States for years, became suspect after the United States entered the war. So did all things German. In 1917, the United States had a population of about 10 million Americans of German ancestry; another 1.4 million citizens had been born in Germany; and about 500,000 Germans were residents who had not yet become U.S. citizens. German-sounding terms were forbidden and patriotically changed. Thus, "sauerkraut" was called "liberty cabbage," and "German measles" became "liberty measles."

Residents of Berlin, New Hampshire, were so worried about their town's name being unpatriotic that they voted on whether to change it; the name Berlin survived, 933 votes to 566. These were harmless reactions to the war, but unfortunately some people also discriminated against those of German ancestry, and laws and regulations were passed that restricted their freedom. People with German-sounding names might be called Huns (a derogatory term for Germans) or "kaiser lovers." Gangs sometimes attacked German-Americans and beat them. Some communities established nightly curfews for German-Americans and restricted their right to travel.

Publisher Oscar Ameringer, who had been born in Germany, wrote years later that it had saddened him to see Americans reject German culture by breaking Beethoven's records, burning German books, and prohibiting people from speaking or learning German. He wrote of the lynching in Illinois in April 1918 of a German-American named Robert Prager by a mob of vigilantes who felt he was unpatriotic because he was not in the army. Ameringer wrote, "[They] hanged [Prager] to a tree in Collinsville, Illinois, until he was dead, and later ransacking the room of the corpse for pro-Kaiser evidence, the executioners found that their victim had been refused service in the American army for physical defects." The ringleaders of the mob were charged but acquitted in a trial on the grounds the lynching was a "patriotic murder."

Ameringer also recalled a German-American friend, a veteran of the Civil War, who was taken from his Milwaukee home by a citizens' group because he could not produce his naturalization papers. Ameringer said this elderly man, who had been wounded while fighting for the Union, was fingerprinted and branded an "enemy alien." Officials across the nation often turned their backs when immigrants sought protection from such incidents. This was the case when the Los Angeles police failed to protect Mexican-Americans from the violence directed against them after release of the Zimmermann message.

Immigrants and people with "foreign"-sounding surnames were often charged for statements or incidents that seemed to have no real bearing on the war. For example, Ricardo Flores Magon, a Mexican-American labor organizer in the Southwest, was sentenced to twenty years in prison for criticizing the president's handling of affairs with Mexico. At times, the persecution of immigrants came about because people did not understand either their language or their ethnic backgrounds. In another example, during the war, Czechs living in the United States organized troops to fight against the Central Powers. But their rallies in Iowa and Nebraska were sometimes broken up by people who mistakenly thought the Czechs were trying to enlist soldiers to fight against the Allies. The people breaking up the Czech rallies did not understand the language. They simply assumed that any group of foreign-sounding people who had gathered together were enemies of the United States.

Frederic Howe, director of immigration for New York City during the war, wrote that immigrants at Ellis Island were treated terribly. "[It was] a two-year panic over the 'Hun.' . . . During these years thousands of Germans, Austrians, and Hungarians were taken without trial from their homes and brought to Ellis Island," he wrote later. He added that many people were deported without having done anything wrong. This antiforeign mood led to the passage by Congress on February 5, 1917, of the first of a series of restrictive immigration laws. Congress, over the veto of President Wilson, for the first time imposed a literacy requirement for immigrants older than age sixteen. It also totally prohibited immigration from the so-called Asiatic Barred Zone, which included India, Afghanistan, Arabia, and many smaller Asian countries. Patriotism and the love of country had become an unwitting ally of fear and intolerance.

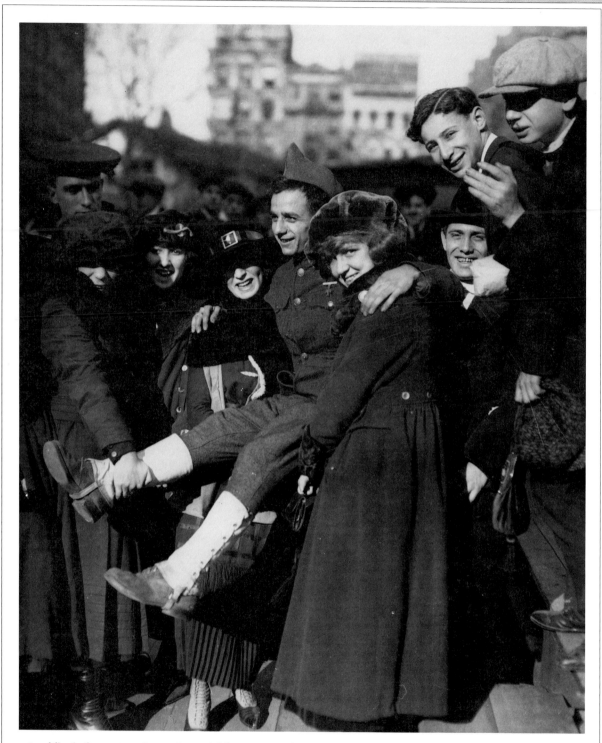

A soldier is the center of attention as jubilant New Yorkers celebrate the end of the Great War on November 11, 1918. Although U.S. civilians never had to endure the brutality of the war, many had made huge sacrifices, including the loss of loved ones killed in battle. People all over the world celebrated the end of this first global conflict.

War's End — 1918

More than two million U.S. soldiers were shipped overseas in the Great War to help forge a victory against the Central Powers. But because it took such a long time to raise and train an army after declaring war in early 1917, only eighty-five thousand soldiers had arrived in France by March of 1918 when Germany started its final great offensive of the war. Russia's exit from the war had allowed the Central Powers to transfer nearly a half-million soldiers to the Western Front. On March 21, the Germans launched a massive attack to start the Second Battle of the Somme. The Germans gained more territory in five days than either side had since Germany's own lightning strike into France at the start of the war. Germany launched two more successful attacks on the Western Front, seizing more ground before halting in early June to regroup. Although successful in its three offensives, Germany had sustained some eight hundred thousand casualties, the total of those who were both wounded and killed. The Allies also suffered great losses, but by June, more than three hundred thousand U.S. soldiers were landing in France every month. These troops would tip the balance of military strength in the Allies' favor. The Germans attacked again in July in the Second Battle of the Somme. This time, however, the Allies, backed by the United States, were too strong and stopped the advance.

The Allies then began to drive against the Germans, and by August, they had begun pushing the German lines back. On August 8, the British, with help from Canadian and Australian troops, struck the Germans north and south of the Somme River. Eventually, at the Battle of Amiens, the Germans were overwhelmed. The British took twenty-one thousand prisoners, and several German divisions fled in panic. German General Erich Ludendorff called it "the black day of the German Army." He later said that was the point at which he realized his country was doomed and "the war must be ended." But the Allies kept hammering at the Germans along the Western Front and by early September had pushed them back behind the lines they had occupied before their March offensives.

Led by General Pershing, the U.S. forces played a major role in the final

Warfare takes to the air

In 1917, the United States had very few planes and limited experience in aerial combat. But Congress appropriated $640 million for the new U.S. Air Service, and by the end of the war, there were eleven thousand pilots, forty-three hundred of them flying in France.

Eddie Rickenbacker, a former race car driver, shot down twenty-six enemy planes to become the United States' most celebrated flier. The most feared German pilot was Baron Manfred von Richthofen, who won the nickname the "Red Baron."

There was only one African-American pilot in the war, and he flew for France. He was Eugene Bullard, nicknamed "The Black Swallow of Death." Born a slave in Georgia, Bullard hated the way he was treated in the United States because of his race and had moved to France. He joined the French Flying Corps when the war started.

When the United States entered the war, it extended an invitation to Americans flying for the French to join the United States as officers. The offer was accepted by the nearly two hundred Americans who had been flying with the Lafayette Escadrille, a unit of the French Flying Corps made up of U.S. volunteers. Bullard at first agreed to fly for the United States, but U.S. officials refused to make him an officer because he was an African-American. Angered at this racial slight, Bullard continued to fly for the French. He won many medals, including the Croix de Guerre.

At the beginning of the Great War, airplanes were more of a novelty than a weapon. Their main use was for aerial observation, and in 1914, military authorities had greater faith in balloons or Zeppelins (airships with a rigid structure), both of which were able to fly because they were filled with lighter-than-air gas. In 1915, German Zeppelins bombed British towns and cities — the first time such warfare had ever been conducted. Both sides quickly realized the effectiveness of aerial bombing and began using both Zeppelins and airplanes to bomb the enemy.

When the war started, pilots were armed with only pistols and shotguns. After both sides learned to synchronize machine guns with airplane propellers, aircraft became a much more effective weapon. Airplanes could be used to shoot down enemy planes or to kill ground troops. This development was one of the major steps in making airplanes a powerful military weapon.

Sergeant Alvin York used his sharpshooting skills to become one of the biggest heroes of the war.

battles of the war. From June 6 to July 1, about 27,500 Americans fought in the Third Battle of the Aisne, with their fiercest action at Belleau Woods. The Second Battle of the Marne, from July 18 to August 6, is considered a turning point in Allied fortunes. The arrival of more than 350,000 U.S. troops helped turn the tide in this key conflict. The Germans had mounted an offensive on both sides of the Rheims River, but the Allies stopped them. The Allies' final offensive began on September 6, when U.S. forces were given the task of advancing across the difficult terrain of the Argonne Forest. The combined Allied drive against the German front stretched west from Ypres to Verdun. Although the fighting was slow and bloody, the Allies made steady progress in breaking through the Germans' front lines and pushing them back.

One of the heroes in the final months of war was Alvin York. His platoon was fighting in the Argonne Forest, when it was lured into an ambush by German soldiers, who pretended to surrender but then opened fire on the Americans. Six of the sixteen men in York's unit were killed and three wounded. York, who in his native Tennessee had done a lot of hunting, took up a position about forty yards away from the machine gun nest that had opened fire. Using what he called "good old turkey shooting," he started picking off the Germans. He killed all eight men in the gun crew, and his deadly sharpshooting so unnerved the rest that they surrendered. York and the remaining men in his unit captured 132 prisoners, including a major. York is generally considered the biggest U.S. hero of the war, but there were thousands of soldiers of all walks of life who fought bravely for the United States.

Knowing they were beaten, the Germans on October 3 sent a diplomatic note to President Woodrow Wilson requesting an armistice (an agreement to suspend fighting) and asking for peace negotiations based on his Fourteen Points (which will be discussed later in this chapter). While both sides traded diplomatic messages and tried to agree on key issues, the fighting continued for more than a month. That meant tens of thousands more soldiers had to die before terms of the armistice were worked out. German Kaiser Wilhelm II finally abdicated on November 9. Two days later on November 11, the guns fell silent in Europe for the first time since July 28, 1914.

The War Ends around the Globe

Although the most dramatic fighting occurred in Europe on the Eastern and Western Fronts, the Great War was one that engulfed the world as it spread to European-controlled colonies in Africa, Asia, and the Middle East. In 1918, the conflict came to a close on those faraway battlefields as well.

Bulgaria, still fighting on the side of the Central Powers, waged a battle against Serbian, French, and Greek forces in 1918 before finally agreeing to an armistice September 29, more than a month before Germany surrendered. Austria-Hungary, which had started the war at the prompting of Germany, had struggled for five years to do its share of the fighting against mostly Russian, Italian, and Serbian armies. Austria-Hungary had fought well against Italy, but on October 24 — the anniversary of its huge loss at Caporetto — Italy launched a major offensive with the help of British troops. Within a few days, this onslaught had broken the spirit of the Austro-Hungarian army. Its soldiers mutinied, and on October 28, the Austrian high command ordered a retreat. By November 3, Austria-Hungary had requested and won an armistice, a condition of which was that Austrian Emperor Charles would give up his throne. He stepped down on November 11 to end the long reign of the Hapsburgs, a royal German family that had ruled in Austria since 1278.

Throughout the Great War, the Turkish Ottoman Empire had ably defended its territory in Europe as well as its holdings in the Middle East. Here, the fighting had been much different

The armistice came twice

News of the end of the Great War was joyously celebrated in the United States. In fact, thanks to one of the biggest mistakes in journalism history, Americans got to celebrate the end of the war *twice.*

On November 7, 1918, United Press, a news service with reporters in Europe covering the war, sent a bulletin from France to newspapers in the United States saying the war had ended. Afternoon newspapers carried the story, and as word spread, there was a joyous celebration throughout the country. People crowded into the streets of big cities, rang church bells, and celebrated the best news in years.

At that time, there were no television cameras to relay images of news events as they took place or even live radio reports. The news was sent by telegraph, and it was a slow process to get news stories from Europe. But when several hours went by and no other news agency had reported the armistice, journalists — and then the entire nation — began to suspect something might be wrong.

As it turned out, the story was wrong. Roy Howard, president of United Press, had been shown a dispatch by Admiral H. B. Wilson that had just been sent from Paris. It said: "Armistice signed this morning at 11 — all hostilities cease at 2:00 P.M. today." Howard, like any good reporter who thought he had a scoop, filed his story. But the announcement was false and the celebration it touched off back home was premature, although not for very long. When the armistice was officially announced on November 11, the nation went wild with joy all over again.

And the war was really over.

Lawrence of Arabia

T. E. Lawrence is better known in history as Lawrence of Arabia, the British scholar-soldier who helped lead Arabs in battle against the fading Ottoman Empire. In a conflict best remembered for the horrors of the trenches and poison gas, his exploits in the Middle East carried a sense of daring and romance that made him one of the war's greatest heroes.

Lawrence had spent the years before the war in Palestine (present-day Israel) doing archaeological research and studying the language and culture of Arab tribes, who were ruled by the Turks. When the war began, he made maps for the British Army of the desert land he knew so well. But when his two brothers were killed in battle in France, Lawrence decided he wanted to join the fighting in the Middle East. He became a liaison between the British forces and the Arabs as they battled Turkey. He helped develop the hit-and-run guerrilla tactics that crippled the Turkish armies.

Amir is an Arabic term for "leader." The mounted guerrilla fighters Lawrence led affectionately called him "Amir Dynamite" for his daring plans to destroy bridges and supply trains. Wearing the flowing robes of the Arabs and mounted on a camel, Lawrence led troops into battle. He did not just give orders but took part in the fighting. In the process, he became a legend.

In 1917, Lawrence was captured by the Turks and tortured. He eventually escaped and continued to fight against them. He marched into Damascus with the victorious Arab forces in October 1918 at the end of fighting in the Middle East. He also served as interpreter and adviser for Arab leaders at the Paris peace talks after the war, cutting a dashing, exotic figure in his Arab garb. He is shown at the peace talks in the photo above, middle row.

than in Europe. In the vast desert regions, both sides had to depend on cavalry units instead of cars and trucks. They rode either horses or camels into battle. Turkey's main foe in the Middle East was the British, and in the final year of the war, it became clear that the Turks were fighting a losing battle. On October 1, British and Arab forces captured Damascus (a city in the nation known today as Syria) at the same time they were making great gains in Mesopotamia (known today as Iraq). The Turkish government realized it was losing the battle in the Middle East. It also knew if it lost, Turkey's eastern borders would be left defenseless and open to attack by the Allies. Because of that fear, the Ottoman Empire surrendered and signed an armistice on October 30.

The Human Cost of the Great War

The Great War caused the most deaths of any war up until that time in history. The Allied Powers had mobilized more than 42 million soldiers, while the Central Powers fielded nearly 23 million. The Allies reported 5.1 million "killed and died," and the Central Powers nearly 3.4 million, for a total of more than 8.5 million deaths caused by military action or disease during the war.

German soldiers, their arms raised, are searched for hidden weapons after surrendering to British troops. Near the end of the Great War, German troops were so demoralized that they often surrendered willingly.

The Allies also had more than 12.8 million wounded soldiers and the Central Powers nearly 8.4 million. At the end of the war, the Allies designated 4.1 million soldiers "prisoners and missing" and the Central Powers more than 3.6 million. Many of those soldiers probably died, but authorities were never able to verify their deaths. The United States, which fought for only part of the war, suffered 116,516 deaths, and more than 204,000 U.S. soldiers were wounded. By contrast, in World War II, more than 16 million Americans served in the armed forces and 292,131 were killed; worldwide at least 46 million people lost their lives in this second great global conflict.

Artillery, that is, heavy guns or cannons, caused the most deaths and wounds, followed by small arms and poison gas. More soldiers on both sides died from poor medical treatment and disease than were killed as a direct cause of battle. For example, thousands of U.S. soldiers also died in the influenza epidemic that hit Europe and the United States so hard in 1918. The illness started in Europe, and there was speculation that it had been brought there by the two hundred thousand laborers imported from China to help in the war effort. Almost on-half million people in the United States died in this epidemic, which also swept through army camps overseas and in the United States. Many soldiers listed as killed in the war actually died from this disease.

The fighting spread to civilian areas in many parts of the world, bringing with it death and destruction on a scale never seen before — or even contemplated in anyone's worst nightmares. Estimates of the number of civilian deaths resulting from the Great War vary, but it is believed that as many as 22 million lost their lives. They died from starvation, exposure, disease, military encounters, and massacres.

Woodrow Wilson: Peacemaker, Visionary

The fighting ended when Germany and the other defeated nations signed the armistice, an agreement to suspend fighting. However, the nations involved in the Great War still had to negotiate peace treaties to formally end the war. At this point, the world turned expectantly to President Woodrow Wilson. Even before the United States entered the war, Wilson had spoken about his vision

President Woodrow Wilson addresses Congress in July of 1918. One of the most brilliant speakers ever elected president, Wilson is remembered for many memorable speeches.

Fierce nationalists

Among the strongest believers in nationalism were Czechs, South Slavs (called Yugoslavs), and Poles. The Czechs had long been restless at being ruled by Austria-Hungary, and in 1916, Tomas Masaryk (a Slovak) and Edvard Benes organized a Czechoslovak National Council. The two had both left the war-torn area that was their homeland. They met with Allied leaders and tried to persuade them to create a new country after the war, called Czechoslovakia. The Allies backed this idea, partly in hopes that it would create internal unrest in Austria-Hungary. If Czechs and Slovaks thought an Allied victory would benefit them, maybe they would fight against the Central Powers, as many did, or at least not help the Central Powers in the war. In the same way, Slavic groups in Austria-Hungary hoped for support for a new nation of their own. They formed a group called the Yugoslav Committee, which was based in Paris so it could try to persuade Allied leaders that a nation called Yugoslavia should be created after the war.

When the Great War started, Poles at first did not know whether the Central Powers or the Allies would help them the most in their fight for a free Poland. At the beginning of the twentieth century, their country was divided, with parts of it ruled by Germany, Austria-Hungary, or Russia. But they decided to join the Allies for two reasons: Wilson's emphasis on nationalism, later embodied in his Fourteen Points, and the Bolshevik Revolution in Russia. This upheaval resulted in Russia's agreeing to independence for the part of Poland it controlled. In 1917, Polish exiles in France organized a Polish army to fight against the Central Powers.

of a peace that would last forever. He was considered a leader who could bring about a fair and just end to the bitter war. On January 22, 1917, before the United States had joined the war, Wilson had addressed the U.S. Senate in a speech intended for nations who were fighting. One of the great phrasemakers in presidential history, Wilson stressed that any negotiated end to the war should be a "peace without victory" because only "a peace between equals can last."

On January 8, 1918, Wilson outlined his famous Fourteen Points as the "only possible program" for peace. It stressed that peace terms must be "openly arrived at" and that the world's seas must be free and open to everyone in the future. There were specific demands concerning the future of some lands currently ruled by others — for instance, a free and independent Poland would be created — and nations would generally have to leave territory they had occupied during the war.

Several of his points centered on the right of nations and ethnic groups to determine who should govern them.

Point number five, for example, called for a fair adjustment of colonial claims that would balance the interests of the population with those of the government. Number ten sought opportunity for the peoples of Austria-Hungary to govern themselves. Number twelve made a similar recommendation for nationalities under Turkish rule.

One of his most important recommendations was point number fourteen. In it, Wilson proposed "a general association of nations to be formed under specific covenants for the purpose of affording mutual guarantees of political independence and territorial integrity to great and small states alike." This proposal gave rise to the League of Nations, which, after World War II, evolved into the international organization known today as the United Nations.

In another speech on February 11, Wilson elaborated on his stand concerning self-determination. The president said, "National aspirations must be respected: peoples may now be dominated and governed only by their own consent. 'Self-determination' is not a mere phrase; it is an imperative principle of action." Wilson's plea for independence and freedom for areas that had been ruled by force in the past was received with joy around the world. The war was still going on, but many oppressed groups throughout the world heard Wilson's words and took heart. Among them were Czechs, Slovaks, Croats, Serbs, and other ethnic groups in Austria-Hungary; Arabs fighting Turkish rule in the Middle East; Africans whose homelands were ruled by European powers; and Poles whose homeland was divided into areas governed by both Russia and Germany. Wilson had positively inflamed the rising tide of nationalism already sweeping the world, igniting a new desire for freedom among many peoples.

Jews suffer in the Russian Revolution

In March 1917, Czar Nicholas II of Russia stepped down, ending the Romanov dynasty. When he did, Jews in Russia had hoped conditions would improve for them in a country where they had been persecuted and brutally killed by the thousands for centuries.

Russia had seen repeated pogroms — race riots in which Jews were attacked and killed. Many Russians held deep-rooted feelings of anti-Semitism (prejudice against Jews) that resulted in laws restricting the rights of Jews. At the time of the Great War, Jewish people faced similar discrimination in other European countries and even the United States. But it was worse in Russia than almost any place else.

In October 1917, the Bolshevik (Communist) Party wrested control of the provisional government organized after Nicholas had abdicated the throne. The Jews expected better treatment. Although the Bolsheviks rescinded anti-Semitic laws, Jewish merchants were among the first of the so-called anti-social groups they attacked. Many Jews were killed or exiled to the remote region of Siberia; many others simply fled the country. The Bolsheviks, who opposed any kind of religion, also tried to stamp out the Jewish faith by closing almost all synagogues and prohibiting the study of Hebrew (the language of their religious services) or the publication of anything in Hebrew.

In 1918, the Bolsheviks began fighting a civil war against the White Armies. These opponents, many of them members of Russian royalty, were trying to overthrow the communists, who were known as Reds. The White forces considered all Jews their enemies because some Bolshevik leaders were Jewish. Because of this, many Jews were killed during the civil war between the Whites and the Reds.

It is estimated that more than one thousand separate incidents involving the killing of Jews took place during this period and that as many as sixty to seventy thousand Jews died. The identification of Jews with communism spread to other Eastern European countries at this time and led to more anti-Semitic attacks, especially in the countries known today as Poland and Hungary.

Seated from left to right are the "Big Four" leaders who dominated the peace talks to end the Great War — Vittorio Orlando (Italy), David Lloyd George (Britain), Georges Clemenceau (France), and Woodrow Wilson (United States). Clemenceau and Lloyd George bitterly hated Germany and fought to make terms of the Treaty of Versailles as harsh as possible.

CHAPTER SIX

Aftermath of War: The World and America, 1919

When President Woodrow Wilson proclaimed an era of "self-determination" for all peoples who wished to govern their own lives, his words stirred passions of nationalism in places he could hardly have imagined. One of those places was a tiny village in the mountains of northern Austria, where a small pocket of Polish farmers lived. They were upset about national borders being drawn up that would place them in the new nation of Czechoslovakia. They wanted to live in Poland, another new nation being created in the peace terms to settle the war, because they wanted to be governed by other Poles. So two peasant farmers and a priest, who, luckily, spoke French, made their way down out of the mountains and walked hundreds of miles to the French capital. They wanted to appeal directly to the American president who had said all people should have the right to determine who would govern them.

This tiny delegation tracked Wilson down at his hotel and met with him briefly. But the president really could not help them because, after all, it was impossible to satisfy the wishes of everyone in creating a new world order. Yet that is exactly what the world expected from Wilson and other leaders. The peace talks began January 18, 1919, and ran through June 28 — ironically, the fifth anniversary of the assassination of Archduke Franz Ferdinand and his wife.

Japan comes to the peace talks

The island nation of Japan went to the Paris peace talks looking for respect and for territory. It went away with far less land than it hoped for — and a slap in the face from European nations on the subject of racial equality.

For the most part, Asian nations considered the Great War a "civil war" among Europeans, but Japan had viewed it as a chance to win new territory. When the Great War started, Japan declared war on Germany and easily defeated its military forces to win control of the Shantung area in China. During the war, Japan also sent ships to Europe to help the Allies in their antisubmarine operations. So Japan went to the peace talks expecting to be treated as a valuable ally and to be given the land it felt it needed to grow stronger.

The Allies did give Japan former German-owned islands in the Pacific north of the equator, which proved to be important military bases for Japan during World War II. But the Japanese were denied German holdings in Shantung, which offended them.

The Japanese also failed in their attempt to have a resolution included in the League of Nations' covenant to recognize the principle of racial equality. President Wilson helped draft the resolution Japan wanted, but other allies pressured him into accepting a compromise. The watered-down resolution endorsed only "the principle of the equality of nations and just treatment of their nationals." It did not state in the more forceful terms that Japan wanted that all races were equal — a statement the white, European-dominated conference would not accept. Even the weaker version was passed by only a small majority.

Japan went away from the peace talks nursing a grudge over what had happened and still seeking expansion in Asia. Its ambitions to control more territory led to further aggression against China in the 1920s and 1930s and eventually its attack on Pearl Harbor in Hawaii in 1941. And the bombing of Hawaii was the incident that pushed the United States into its second world war.

Wilson's idealistic vision of a peace that would make the Great War "the war to end all wars" had created unbelievably high expectations for people around the world. He had given new hope to people who wanted to govern their own affairs, whether it was an entire nation dominated by another country or a handful of Poles who wanted to live in Poland.

The talks, held in Paris, led to decisions that dismantled the Austro-Hungarian, German, and Ottoman Empires. Nine new, independent nations were created in Europe, but the European colonial empires in other parts of the world were left intact: Central Power colonies were simply handed over to various Allied nations. Thus, millions of people in Africa, the Middle East, Asia, and other parts of the world failed to win any new freedom. Even more sadly, the war that was supposed to be the last one ever had to be given a new name in only twenty years — World War I — because it was followed by a second worldwide conflict called World War II.

The Paris peace talks were dominated by Wilson, David Lloyd George of Great Britain, Georges Clemenceau of France, and Vittorio Orlando of Italy. Collectively, these leaders of the Allied nations became known as the "Big Four." But officials from nearly every country in the world had gathered in Paris for the talks, and other Allied nations, such as Japan and Belgium, were consulted in some of the decisions. Also, representatives from other countries, ethnic groups, or nationalities had an opportunity to state their views at the negotiations. They brought pleas for racial equality, freedom from foreign domination, suggestions for redrawing boundary lines for new nations, and appeals for protection from attacks by other ethnic or national groups in their own country.

The United States had provided the winning edge in the war, but Wilson found himself outmatched by Allied leaders as he tried to create the kind of peace he envisioned. When the Germans agreed to quit fighting, they had thought the peace terms would be based on Wilson's Fourteen Points. But the countries of Lloyd George, Clemenceau, and Orlando had suffered much more in the war than the United States. These leaders were bent on exacting revenge and compensation from Germany. Said Clemenceau, "The greater the bloody catastrophe which devastated and ruined one of the richest regions of France, the more ample and splendid should be the reparation." During the months that the talks were held, Clemenceau and Lloyd George periodically toured nearby battlefields, as if to refresh their minds with the horrors of the war and harden their hearts anew.

Wilson, unable to withstand this burning hatred and fierce desire for revenge, made many compromises during the long, drawn-out talks. He agreed to harsher peace terms for Germany than he thought were necessary, gave in on disputes over borders for new nations, and allowed his goal of "self-determination" for all nations to be weakened. And the Allies, except for the United States, fought among themselves to acquire territory being taken away from Germany.

Ho Chi Minh at the peace talks

One of the petitioners in Paris was Ho Chi Minh of Vietnam, who, with two of his countrymen, had drawn up an eight-point plan to end colonial domination of his homeland. France controlled not only Vietnam but several other areas in what was then known as Indochina. When Ho was denied a chance to plead for freedom for Vietnam, he began writing articles about Indochina to publicize its plight to the world. He also joined the French Socialist party. Thus began a political career that culminated in his leading the armed fight in the 1950s that freed Vietnam from French rule. When Vietnam was split into two countries by the United Nations, he was elected the leader of North Vietnam, a communist country. In the early 1970s, North Vietnam won a war with the United States, which allowed it to take control of South Vietnam and unify the entire nation.

Wilson gave in so often because he wanted to insure that the peace terms would include the covenant of the League of Nations — the global body he thought idealistically, could insure peace for all time. The league was established in the treaty, but Wilson, its creator, was never able to win acceptance of the league in the United States. So just as Germany lost the war, Wilson lost the peace, or at least the kind of peace he had hoped to achieve.

The peace terms are called the Treaty of Versailles because they were signed June 28, 1919, in the Hall of Mirrors in Versailles, the historic palace of French emperors. Germany was not allowed to participate in the talks. It simply had to accept the conditions the Allies decided on. The Germans, officials and citizens alike, hated the treaty. One official said the treaty meant "the annihilation of Germany." The Treaty of Versailles deals only with Germany, but at the peace talks in Paris, Allied leaders made decisions concerning treaties that were eventually signed by other Central Powers.

Russia was also not invited to the negotiations. Russia had been a valuable partner of the Allies for most of the Great War and suffered more deaths (1.7 million) in fighting than any other nation except Germany. European nations turned against Russia for two reasons. The first is that when the communists came to power in the Bolshevik Revolution in October of 1917, Russia quit fighting. The new Russian government declared an armistice in December and a few months later agreed to peace terms with Germany in the Treaty of Brest-Litovsk. Because the Russians were no longer fighting, the Germans were able to shift one-half million soldiers to the Eastern Front for the final year of the war. This greatly strengthened Germany, prolonging the war and leading to more deaths for the Allied forces. The second reason is that European nations were frightened of communism, which opposed their own capitalist economic systems.

The Peace Treaties

The Treaty of Versailles was actually a collection of individual treaties that were agreed upon by the participating Allies. These treaties covered a range of military and political issues, among them the establishment of a League of Nations, the punishment to be dealt Germany, the establishment of new nations following the war, and the carving up of Turkey's Ottoman Empire into smaller — and weaker — segments. The following summarizes the main points of these treaties.

Covenant of the League of Nations. The Treaty of Versailles created the framework for the league, which was designed as an organization where nations could meet to resolve their conflicts. After World War II, the League of Nations, which had proven unsuccessful in dealing with world problems, was disbanded. It was replaced by the United Nations.

Germany. Germany was ordered to pay fifty-six billion dollars in reparations to the Allied nations. These payments crippled Germany's economy and caused the economic and social unrest that helped elevate Adolf Hitler to power in the 1930s. Germany was also stripped of about 10 percent of its land in Europe, with bits and pieces given to France, Poland, and other countries. Its colonies in China, the Pacific, and Africa were also given to Allied nations. The treaty terms also limited the size of German defense forces.

New Nations. Nine new nations were created, with four of them coming from the former Austro-Hungarian Empire. Bosnia, Herzegovina, Croatia, and Slovenia were merged with Serbia and Montenegro to become Yugoslavia; Hungary became an independent nation; the Czechs and Slovaks, two dominant ethnic groups, were placed together in Czechoslovakia; and the small area left, which had about six million German-speaking people, became Austria. Poland,

A turning point for Hitler

When the Great War finally came to an end, Adolf Hitler was a patient recuperating from a poison gas attack in a military hospital near Berlin. On November 10, 1918, Hitler and other wounded German soldiers were told that Germany had surrendered. The news affected him so greatly that he lost control of his emotions. "I could stand it no longer. Everything went black before my eyes," he later wrote. Hitler even admitted he cried for the first time since his mother had died when he was a child.

After a long period of sorrow and anger over his country's defeat, Hitler made a choice that would lead to another war and even greater misery for the world. "My own fate became known to me. I, for my part, decided to go into politics," he said. Thus, Hitler set himself on the course to win political control of Ger-

many, a course that would eventually lead to World War II.

Hitler had enjoyed being a soldier. Not even the horrors of trench warfare bothered him, although some soldiers who fought with him remembered him as an odd comrade. Hitler, they said, sat and brooded in silence for long periods of time. Then, he would jump up and give a speech blaming "the Jews and the Marxists" for all of Germany's problems.

After the war, Hitler first started attracting followers by giving speeches throughout Germany. He attacked the Treaty of Versailles and still blamed others for the fact that his country had lost the war. It was the resentment and hatred that Hitler evoked in his fellow citizens that, more than anything else, led Germany into starting another world war just two decades later.

which before the war had been divided into areas ruled by Germany and Russia, was given its independence. Poland also received West Prussia, Posen, and parts of Upper Silesia from Germany and was guaranteed a corridor to the Baltic Sea through Germany. Three more nations that emerged from the peace talks were the Baltic States — Latvia, Lithuania, and Estonia — which formerly had been controlled by Russia. Finland also won its freedom from Russia.

Ottoman Empire. The Allies had already carved up the Ottoman Empire in secret treaties agreed on during the war, but final details of the Treaty of Sevres were not worked out until 1920. This treaty was named after the French city in which it was signed. Almost all of the Arabic-speaking part of the

Palestine and the Jewish homeland

One of the decisions made at the Paris peace talks was to have Great Britain take temporary control of the land that became modern-day Israel. Great Britain's mandate was to turn the former Ottoman Empire possession into a national homeland for Jews such as those shown here in Palestine. There was only one problem — somebody already lived there.

When the Great War was over, Jews and Arabs both lived on those lands, and both wanted Palestine to be given to them. Great Britain confused both sides by making conflicting promises about the territory. As a result, Jews and Arabs began to fight each other for control of Palestine. In 1919, Bedouin (nomadic Arab) tribes attacked Jewish settlements in the region of the Upper Galilee, and on April 4, 1920, Arabs began three days of rioting against Jews in Jerusalem.

Great Britain finally decided to honor the Balfour Agreement, the name for the order that Palestine become a Jewish homeland. In 1920, it allowed 16,500 Jews from Europe and other countries to immigrate to Palestine. This angered Arabs, who responded in May 1921 with anti-Jewish riots that killed 46 Jewish people and wounded 146. Despite the Arab opposition, the League of Nations in 1922 affirmed the British mandate for Palestine.

Palestine did not become a free Jewish nation until after World War II. Tragically, decades after Israel had become a nation recognized by most of the nations of the world, Arabs and Jews are still fighting over control of parts of Palestine.

Ottoman Empire was put under the control of France and Great Britain. Arabia remained independent, although its monarchies were still dependent on Great Britain. The Ottoman Empire was also forced to give up some islands and land in Europe, to allow Armenia to become an independent nation, and to open the Dardanelles Straits to world navigation.

After the Great War, nationalist fervor, which Wilson himself had helped spur, led to armed revolts in many areas controlled by European countries. In India, the Hindu nationalist Mohandas Karamchand Gandhi emerged to lead the fight for freedom from Great Britain. Gandhi was a former moderate who had helped the British recruit troops in India to fight in the Great War. After the war, Gandhi became angry because Great Britain continued to rule his country as it always had. He had hoped for more freedom for his nation as acknowledgment for the help it gave Great Britain during the war. This disappointment motivated Ghandi to start the peaceful campaign that led to his country becoming an independent nation in 1947. The desire for freedom from British rule also spread to Africa, although it took many more years for those colonies to win their freedom. The Middle East was also the scene of nationalist revolts as former Ottoman Empire territories fought to become independent. Eventually, the nations of Israel, Iraq, Lebanon, and Syria emerged from those former Turkish lands.

Wilson's Failure at Home

When President Wilson returned home in July 1919, he attempted to win approval of the Treaty of Versailles from a hostile U.S. Senate. Republican senators did not like the treaty and they did not like Wilson. Even though he was a Democrat, in the interests of U.S. solidarity, Republican leaders had loyally backed him during the war. But in October 1918, he angered them when he appealed to citizens to vote only for Democrats in the congressional elections. Wilson had argued that Democratic losses would be "interpreted on the other side of the water [Europe] as a repudiation" of his leadership, thus weakening the U.S. position in bringing the war to a close. He also snubbed Republicans by taking only one Republican to the peace talks. Wilson's use of the ongoing war as a political weapon angered voters as well. In November, Wilson, who himself had been elected by the narrowest of margins only two years earlier, saw the nation elect Republican majorities in both the House and Senate.

The Senate opposed the League of Nations for a variety of reasons. Many Republicans simply did not want the United States to become too heavily involved in world affairs. Some senators were also jealous that Wilson, a Demo-

The battle between management and labor

In the period after the Great War, the United States went through an economic slowdown. This usually happens after a war because all the businesses that have been manufacturing and selling war supplies suddenly have no customers. Because of this slowdown, many companies started laying off workers. During the war, many African-Americans, other minorities, and women had gotten good jobs for the first time in their lives. Now, they were among the first to be let go.

Complicating this situation was the fact that in the postwar period, the battle between business management and labor unions heated up again. The unions were trying to win better conditions for workers. Businesses retaliated by trying to connect labor unions to communism as a tactic to make the general public reject the unions. In one notorious example, in September 1919, more than 340,000 employees of U.S. Steel went on strike for an eight-hour day and better pay. The giant company took out newspaper ads claiming that communists were responsible for the strike. One ad said, "Stand by America, Show up the Red Agitator."

U.S. Steel and Bethlehem Steel, where the strike soon spread, hired strikebreakers to harass and beat up striking workers. Finally, police and soldiers were called in to disperse striking workers at various plants. Eighteen strikers were killed in the resulting violence. Labor resorted to propaganda techniques, as well. In one instance, Casimir Mazurek, a Polish immigrant who had fought for the United States in the Great War, was killed in one of the strikes in 1919. A labor newspaper stated that Mazurek was "shot to death by hirelings and thugs of the Lackawanna Steel Company because he fearlessly stood for industrial democracy on American soil."

Labor and management were completely at odds in these disputes. Workers, who had refrained from striking and worked long hours during the Great War to help achieve victory, felt they had a right to fight for a better life. Workers in this postwar period often had to work ten hours a day, six days a week, and they had few benefits. But owners of factories and other businesses claimed workers were un-American for trying to dictate wages and working conditions. Unfortunately, the disputes between labor and business continued to be violent for many years.

crat, had become so well known all over the world as a peacemaker. They resented the league because Wilson was its chief creator. Senate opposition was so stiff that on September 3, Wilson began a nationwide tour by railroad to build support for the treaty. For Wilson, it was a trip that ended in tragedy. He had never been very strong physically, and the war years and marathon peace talks had weakened him further. On September 26, while traveling to Wichita, Kansas, for another speech, Wilson suffered a stroke that left him in poor condition. He had trouble talking, one side of his face had gone slack, and his left arm and leg would not function properly. The president was rushed back to Washington, where he had another stroke ten days later and was found semiconscious on a bathroom floor in the White House.

Wilson almost died from the second stroke and for several months was an invalid, unable to fulfill most of his duties as president. He made only a partial recovery, and his illness doomed the fight for the treaty. Although Republicans voted the treaty down on November 18, the fighting was over and American troops came home. It was not until July 2, 1921, that the Senate passed a resolution declaring an end to the war between Germany and the United States. The resolution accepted the terms of the Treaty of Versailles, but the Senate still refused to join the League of Nations.

The Great War Reshapes the United States

The Great War was a key period in American history because it marked the nation's debut on the world stage as a major power. The war forever transformed the way other countries viewed and interacted with the United States. The changes created at home, however, were just as important and lasting. But they were mostly negative for African-Americans and other minorities, immigrants, and anyone with political or social ideas that went contrary to majority opinion.

One dramatic incident illustrates the tensions that developed as Americans attempted to adjust to the changes brought by the war years. In June 1919 in Chicago, Eugene Williams went swimming off a beach along Lake Michigan. But the young African-American made a fatal mistake when he crossed over the invisible line into the swimming area reserved for whites. Whites on the beach began stoning Williams for this breach of racial "etiquette," and he drowned. Police refused to make any arrests, and soon people of both races at the beach started fighting. The violence spread throughout the city, and for six days, African-Americans and whites engaged in riots. Thirty-eight people were killed, 537 injured, and more than one thousand homes were destroyed. A grand jury report ruled "the colored people suffered more at the hands of white hoodlums than white people suffered at the hands of black hoodlums." This was just one incident during the summer of 1919, which became known as the "Red Summer." Twenty-eight bloody race riots took place across the nation. Because of the northern migration of African-Americans during the war, racial violence was no longer confined to the South.

In addition to racial tension, the postwar years brought other unrest. There was also a "Red Scare," the term for fear of a communist takeover in the Unit-

Chicago police escort an African-American man to safety during the aftermath of an incident that led to the drowning of a young Black child. Throughout the summer of 1919, race riots broke out in twenty-eight U.S. cities in both the North and South.

ed States like the one that had occurred in Russia. And immigration laws were tightened to keep out "foreigners." Said political commentator Walter Lippman of the nation's postwar mood, "We seem to be the most frightened lot of victors that the world ever saw." There was also an explosion of labor activity; in 1919 alone, for example, more than four million workers took part in four thousand strikes.

The years after the war were especially difficult for African-Americans, including those who had moved north in search of a better life. Black Americans had expected to be rewarded with more equitable treatment after a war in which so many African-American soldiers had fought for their country. In 1919, W. E. B. Du Bois wrote in *Crisis*, the journal of the National Association for the Advancement of Colored People, that African-American soldiers returned to "a land that lynches them, disfranchises them, encourages ignorance, steals from them, insults them, but they do return. We return. We return from fighting. We return fighting. Make way for Democracy! We saved it in France, and by the Great Jehovah, we will save it in the United States of America, or know the reason why." They were brave words, but African-Americans, even when they tried to fight back, were outnumbered.

During the war, many African-Americans had bettered themselves economically by working at new jobs, and thousands of soldiers returned from battle with a new sense of pride in themselves. The bloody events of the Red Summer were seen by some whites as necessary, a lesson to show Blacks that nothing had changed. In the South, there was an increase in the number of lynchings, eighty-three in 1919 alone. Incredibly, some of the African-Americans hanged were former soldiers. Discrimination and violence against Blacks continued for many decades in the United States. It was not until the civil rights movement began gaining strength in the 1950s that Blacks started to win some relief from what African-American leader Dr. Martin Luther King Jr., termed "the manacles of segregation and the chains of discrimination."

In contrast, the Great War was a liberating experience for American women, who began their move out of the kitchen and into the work force of the United States. The war provided thousands of job opportunities for women. By 1918, a million more women were working than before the start of the war. When millions of men were drafted, women were hired for jobs they had never been allowed to try. They worked as streetcar conductors, labored in munitions plants, toiled on farms, and delivered the mail. For the first time, women were even hired by police departments, although they mainly directed traffic and handled clerical duties. A patriotic poster of the time had a woman saying, "Not just hats off to the flag, but sleeves up for it." The message was that women were willing to work hard to win the war. These new jobs gave many women a sense of independence and helped foster the emerging feminist movement.

One woman banking executive said she owed her rise to the war. "It was not until our men were called overseas that we made any real onslaught on the realm of finance," she said, "and became tellers, managers of departments, and junior and senior officers." An African-American woman who went from working as a domestic to a job in the factory, rejoiced in her new position. She vowed, "I'll never work in nobody's kitchen but my own any more."

The new status of women was reflected in their finally winning the right to vote. On January 10, 1918, the U.S. House of Representatives voted 274 to 126 to adopt the Susan B. Anthony amendment to the Constitution, which gave women voting power. The amendment was named for Anthony, a leader in the movement for women's suffrage, or the right to vote. The Senate defeated it by two votes but passed it in 1919. Finally, in 1920, enough states had ratified the amendment to make it the law of the land. Carrie Chapman Catt, president of the national American Woman Suffrage Movement, said the right to vote meant women were no longer "wards of the nation, but free and equal citizens."

During the Great War, the U.S. government had dealt harshly with immigrants and foreign-born citizens who opposed the war, in many cases violating the rights of these Americans in the name of national security. The war had created fear about foreign-born citizens because other Americans had worried, needlessly for the most part, about their loyalty in time of war. Even when the fighting stopped, many Americans still felt negatively about immigrants and began to consider many of them "undesirable." Such feelings were mainly based on race (in the case of Africans and Asians), religion (for Jews, Roman Catholics, and Muslims), and country of origin (for Russia and Eastern European countries). Congress, which in 1917 had already tightened immigration, in 1921 passed a bill setting immigration quotas. Each nationality and ethnic group was allowed a certain number of immigrants every year based on a small, fixed percentage of its total U.S. population as of the 1910 census. The quotas favored groups that had achieved large U.S. populations by 1910, in particular those from Great Britain and Western Europe. The quotas were, in

The United States grows up

The United States entered the twentieth century a young nation, one that was growing in power but still felt awed by the older European cultures. Before the war, the United States was beginning to create its own identity in music, literature, painting, and other areas of the arts. Yet it still followed the creative standards set by Great Britain, Germany, France, and other European countries.

To Americans, culture meant what an artist was painting in Paris, what an author was writing in London, what kinds of music and ballet were being performed in Moscow. Most citizens of this fledgling nation were the descendants of people who had come from those countries. They revered their European heritages and did not feel the United States had achieved such greatness.

But after the war, this changed. The United States had become a political and military power the equal of any other nation in the world. Americans stopped looking to Europe exclusively to shape its culture and began to let its own artists and citizens shape its future. And the world began looking to the United States as the leader in many areas. Social historian Lincoln Steffens wrote that the war had served to spread American culture around the world, including the vibrant new music called jazz. "We found the whole world dancing to American jazz, the Germans, too," he wrote after a postwar visit to Europe. "We went into the war a conceited, but secretly rather humble, second-rate country; we came out self-assured. We had measured ourselves with our European competitors and discovered our competence."

effect, designed to limit immigration from Russia, Eastern Europe, the Middle East, Asia, and Africa.

The government was also harsh in its response to the Red Scare. In 1919, U.S. Attorney General A. Mitchell Palmer began a series of raids on unions and radical groups. These raids resulted in the arrest of thousands of people, most of whom were never found guilty of any crimes. In January alone, nearly six thousand people were arrested, some of them girls as young as fourteen and sixteen, who were charged with supporting the violent overthrow of the government. Nearly anyone whose political views were contrary to those held by government officials could be labeled a "Red" and be in danger of arrest. It was a frightening time for many people.

These restrictive policies, which continued through World War II, were a big change for the United States — a nation, after all, that was made up of immigrants and that for more than one hundred years had opened its arms to newcomers. In the years since World War I, many people have discovered that the United States does not always welcome new people. But even though some immigrants have been met with discrimination and racism, the United States still inspires the dream of freedom and a better life in people all over the world.

More than any other war in the life of this young nation, the Great War challenged the idea of the United States as a place of refuge for the weary and oppressed from other parts of the world. For the first time in its history, the United States found itself forming alliances and antagonisms with an unprecedented array of foreign nations. For the first time, the United States found itself forced to confront the profound effects that actions in other parts of the world could have on its own citizenry. Not since the American Revolution, when patriots lined up against colonists loyal to a "foreign" power — Britain — had it become so clear that foreign roots could still play so visible and persistent a part in the lives of people living in America.

1914   June 28: Austrian Archduke Franz Ferdinand and his wife, Sophie, are assassinated in Sarajevo, the capital of Bosnia, then part of the Austro-Hungarian Empire

July 28: Austria-Hungary declares war on Serbia; the declaration is made by telegram, the first time this communications technology was used for such a purpose

Aug. 4: German infantry invade neutral Belgium

Sept. 6-10: The German advance to Paris is stopped in the Battle of the Marne; the end of the battle marks the beginning of trench warfare as both sides start digging in along what will become the Western Front

Oct. 4: President Wilson designates this day as "Peace Sunday" and asks the nation to pray for peace

1915   Jan. 2: The U.S. Senate passes, but President Wilson vetoes, a bill requiring a literacy test for immigrants; similar bills had been vetoed by previous presidents

April 27-May 1: International Congress of Women at The Hague, Netherlands

May 7: A German submarine sinks the *Lusitania,* which was en route from New York to Liverpool, England; among the 1,198 people who died were 128 Americans

July 29: U.S. Marines land in Haiti

Aug. 4-6: German aircraft bomb English towns; on August 15, aircraft of the Allies bomb Karlsruhe, Germany; this marks the beginning of a new type of aerial warfare

Oct. 15: U.S. bankers sign a loan agreement with France and Great Britain for $500 million, money that is used to purchase war supplies in the United States; the signing takes place in the New York offices of banker J. P. Morgan

1916   Jan. 21: The battle of Verdun begins

March 16: Pancho Villa leads a raid on Columbus, N.M., and the nearby camp of the 13th U.S. Cavalry; nine civilians and eight troopers are killed; Brigadier-General John J. Pershing is ordered to enter Mexico and capture Villa

April 18: The United States demands that Germany end unrestricted submarine warfare, vowing to cut off diplomatic relations if Germany does not

July 1: The Allied offensive begins at the Somme

Aug. 4: The United States signs a treaty with Denmark to purchase the Danish West Indies for $25 million and takes possession of the newly named Virgin Islands on March 31,1917

Nov. 7: President Wilson is reelected on theme "He kept us out of war"; Nov. 29: U.S. military occupation of Santo Domingo (today the Dominican Republic) begins; it lasts until 1924.

1917   Feb. 1: Germany resumes submarine warfare; Feb. 3: President Wilson suspends diplomatic relations with Germany; Feb. 5: Immigration Act passed over the president's veto; it bars some Asians

March 1: Details of the "Zimmermann message" are released by President Wilson; newspaper stories of the message, which encourages Mexico to go to war against the United States, inflame U.S. sentiment against Germany; March 2: Passage of the Jones Act makes Puerto Rico a U.S. territory and its residents U.S. citizens; March 12: Russian Czar Nicholas II agrees to step down, ending the Romanov dynasty; March 16: The U.S. ships *City of Memphis, Illinois,* and *Valencia* are reported sunk by U-boats

April 2 : President Wilson asks Congress for a declaration of war; the Senate approves the war resolution 82-6 with eight abstentions; two days later, the House votes 373-50 in favor of war; April 6: The United States declares war on Germany

May 18: President Wilson signs the bill authorizing a military draft

June 5: Registration Day for the draft; nearly 10 million men sign up; June 13: Major General Pershing and his staff arrive in France; the first U.S. troops arrive there June 26; June 15: Congress approves the Espionage Act to punish people who aid the enemy or commit other disloyal acts

July 14: The House approves spending $640 million for a fleet of airplanes

Oct. 25: President Wilson meets in the White House with one hundred members of the New York State Women's Suffrage Party; he endorses passage of equal suffrage

Dec. 17: The House passes the Eighteenth Amendment to the U.S. Constitution, and one day later the Senate follows suit; the amendment, known as the Prohibition Amendment, still must be ratified by the states before the sale and consumption of alcoholic beverages become illegal in the United States

1918   Jan. 8: President Wilson delivers his Fourteen Points speech, which serves as a framework for peace talks at war's end; Jan. 10: The House, 274-136, adopts the Susan B. Anthony resolution giving women the right to vote, but it fails by two votes in the Senate despite a plea by President Wilson; however, the Senate does pass the resolution in 1919

May 16: The Sedition Act is approved, penalizing those who interfere with the war effort

June 3-6: U.S. troops stop the German advance at Chateau-Thierry and Neuilly

June 6-July 1: U.S. troops take part in the battle of Belleau Wood

July 18-Aug. 6: In the Second Battle of the Marne, the turning point in the war, eighty-five thousand U.S. soldiers take part to stop the German offensive

Nov. 9: German Kaiser Wilhelm II abdicates and flees Germany; Nov. 11: Armistice Day, the end of World War I; this day is celebrated as an annual holiday for the first time one year later; today, it is called Veteran's Day

1919   Jan. 18: President Wilson attends the opening session of the Peace Talks in Paris; Jan. 25-Feb. 14: The covenant of the proposed League of Nations is drafted; President Wilson had insisted it be included in the peace treaty; Jan. 29: The Eighteenth Amendment to the Constitution is ratified, prohibiting the sale of liquor in the United States

June 28: The Treaty of Versailles is signed by Wilson and heads of other nations

July 10-Nov. 19: The Senate considers the Versailles Treaty; finally, it rejects the treaty 55-39 because of opposition to joining the League of Nations; it is not until July 2, 1921, that the Senate will declare a formal end to the war with Germany, accepting all the terms of the Treaty of Versailles but still refusing to join the League of Nations

Sept. 26: President Wilson suffers a stroke while on a tour to build support for the Versailles Treaty; the effects limit his ability to govern for the rest of his term

1920   Aug. 26: Enough states approve the Nineteenth Amendment to the Constitution, giving women the right to vote, to ratify it; women vote in the November presidential election

GLOSSARY

ace   a fighter pilot who has shot down at least five enemy aircraft

A.E.F.   American Expeditionary Force; the title for all U.S. troops sent to Europe to fight in WW I

Allies   also known as the Allied Nations: the United States, Great Britain, France, Italy, Russia, and many other countries who fought the Central Powers in World War I

Bolshevik   the Russian term for communists who took control of Russia in the Bolshevik Revolution in 1917

Central Powers   Germany, Austria-Hungary, Turkey, and Bulgaria: the nations that fought against the Allies

doughboy   military slang for a private soldier first used in the Civil War; it is believed that mounted soldiers called those on foot "adobes" because of earth-colored dust that powdered their uniforms when they followed behind horse units; that word was shortened to "dobes" and then "doughboys"

four-minute men speakers who donated their services to Committee of Public Information propaganda efforts

Jim Crow laws legislation to limit the rights of African-Americans, specifically to segregate them and deny them the right to vote

Kaiser the title for German Emperor Wilhelm II

no man's land The area between opposing trench lines on the Western Front; sometimes this was only twenty to thirty yards wide

slackers men who tried to evade the draft

U-boat a shortened form of *Unterseeboot*, the German word for submarine

victory cabbage a popular term for sauerkraut during the Great War; when the United States went to war against Germany, many German names were patriotically changed or altered

war baby slang term for factories that had huge profits because of the war

war millionaire slang term for businesspeople who profited from war industries

Western Front the line of trenches and defenses the Allies and Central Powers constructed in November and December of 1914 following the Battle of the Marne; running from the North Sea east and south to Switzerland, it was a static battle front for the entire war

"Yellow Peril" fears by whites, based on racial attitudes, of the immigration of Asians to the United States

Zeppelin an airship with a rigid structure powered by motorized propellers and able to fly because it is filled with lighter-than-air gases; they were used in the Great War for aerial bombing missions; named after German Count Ferdinand von Zeppelin, who invented them

FURTHER READING

Fromkin, David. *A Peace to End All Peace: Creating the Modern Middle East 1914-1922.* New York: Henry Holt, 1989.

Lee, Irvin H. *Negro Medal of Honor Men.* New York: Dodd, Mead and Company, 1969.

Little, Arthur W. *From Harlem to the Rhine.* New York: Covici-Friede, 1936.

Meier, Matt S. and Feliciano Ribera. *Mexican Americans/American Mexicans: From Conquistadors to Chicanos.* New York: Hill and Wang, 1993.

Meltzer, Milton. *The Black Americans: A History in Their Own Words.* New York: Thomas Y. Crowell Junior Books, 1984.

Morrow, John H., Jr. *The Great War in the Air: Military Aviation from 1909 to 1921.* Washington: Smithsonian Institution Press, 1993.

Patterson, Charles. *Anti-Semitism: The Road to the Holocaust and Beyond.* New York: Walker and Company, 1982.

Schneider, Dorothy and Carl J. *Into the Breach: American Women Overseas in World War I.* New York: Viking Penguin, 1991.

Shillington, Kevin. *History of Africa.* New York: St. Martin's Press, 1989.

Weatherford, Doris. *American Women's History: An A to Z of People, Organizations, Issues, and Events.* New York: Prentice Hall General Reference, 1994.

Zinn, Howard. *A People's History of the United States.* New York: Harper and Row, 1980.

INDEX